More Than Automobiles
The Packards of Warren, Ohio

by: A.J. Balfour

Dedicated To

My Father and Mother

Who instilled in me a strong
appreciation for the unique
history of our nation and
for those who made it great.

M.T. Publishing Company, Inc.

P.O. Box 6802, Evansville, Indiana 47719-6802
www.mtpublishing.com

Library of Congress Control Number: 2016943108

ISBN: 978-1-945306-11-2

Design by
Alena L. Kiefer
M.T. Publishing Company, Inc.™

Printed in the United States of America.

Table of Contents

Acknowledgments

The story that follows has been developing since 1953 when, at the already car-crazy age of 13, I had my first ride in a brand new Packard Caribbean convertible. A year later my parents grudgingly agreed to let me purchase a run-down 1928 Packard Eight roadster for $200. This completely depleted my savings account which had been carefully built up by paper route earnings. The dizzying spiral into the world of Packard had just begun.

The Packard Motor Car Company ceased operations in Detroit by the college years, but membership in the Society of Automotive Engineers provided exposure to many former Packard employees. The circle of Packard's legacy began widening.

As an owner of vintage Packards, even more contacts developed. One of the most interesting was a man in Warren, Ohio named Terry Martin, who almost single-handedly had taken it upon himself to preserve the history and relics of the Packard presence in the hometown of the Packard automobile. His efforts ultimately resulted in the creation of the National Packard Museum in Warren and the preservation of records and artifacts that arguably make up the best Warren, Ohio Packard collection anywhere.

Terry has generously and openly shared his collection throughout the years. Our mutual love of Packard has been the basis for a continuing friendship for many decades. Much of the material for this book comes from Terry's collection. The story could not have been told without him.

Cindee Mines inside one of the Packard "Twin Cottages," Lakewood, New York.

Terry Martin in 1903 Packard Model F (Old Pacific II), alongside the Ward Packard home in Warren (1983).

The other key figure in this Packard story has been Cindee Mines, a Warren resident with a consuming desire to unfold and document the history of her town. Cindee enthusiastically undertook the tasks of researcher, fact checker, and critic for the story that follows. Her research and travels on behalf of the quest for Packard family knowledge have been exceptional. Much newly discovered information is the direct result of her efforts. Again, this story could not have been told without her.

Many other individuals and organizations should also be recognized for their contribution. With apologies to any that I may have missed, I offer thanks to the following:

Myron Summers, Jan Bland, Elaine McHale – librarian with the Fairfax County Library, Bob Smith, Dan Mathey, National Packard Museum, Wendell Lauth, Lehigh University, Carolyn Packard Limerick, Packard Motor Car Foundation - Packard Proving Grounds, August Thumm, Warren/Trumbull County Public Library, Stuart Blond, Helen Ebersole, Ohio State University, Forest History Society, Federal Bureau of Investigation (FBI), Martha Claire Catlin-historian with the Alexandria Monthly Meeting of the Religious Society of Friends, and Dolly Gilliam.

And finally, I offer eternal thanks and love to Ann, my wife, for all those years that she endured and somehow supported the continuing madness of my Packard hobby. Ann died on 10 December, 2015.

Jim & Ann with friends, in Bob McKeown's 1903 Packard Model F – June, 2015.
Dave Czirr photo

Foreword

For several decades during the 20th century Packard stood at the pinnacle of the worldwide automobile industry, with a product that was routinely chosen by a discriminating clientele who wanted only the best in their motor cars. The Packard family of the 1800's would have been surprised that the world today links their name first and foremost with this form of luxurious transportation.

The Industrial Revolution of the late 19th century had propelled America to a position of world power. Entrepreneurs and capitalists transformed the country with rapidly developing electrification, which in turn reduced the burdens of human labor and provided a rising standard of living for all. The benefits of hard work, personal ingenuity and freedom from oppressive government interference provided great rewards for the nation and for those individuals willing to actively participate in that transformation.

Immediately preceding this Age of Electricity had been a period of invention that more closely bound our vast nation and its commerce.... the steam engine and the railroads that followed were a natural outcome of that time.

Both of the periods of these developments were defining moments for the Packard family of Warren, Ohio. In just two generations the family was able to participate with great success in both of them.

Warren Packard, born in nearby Austintown, was the patriarch of the Packard family line of Warren, Ohio that is the subject of this story. He walked to the village of Warren in 1846 at age eighteen and very soon established himself in the hardware business there. He became involved in many ventures in addition to hardware – there was real estate and a hotel, flagstones, an iron forge and a rolling mill. But the business that contributed most significantly to the early Packard's fortune was lumber-primarily the supply of ties and construction timbers to a rapidly expanding railroad network of the 1860's and '70's. His success closely paralleled the growth and development of America's railroad system.

Warren Packard's five children who reached maturity were thus able to enjoy the prosperity and comfort of a loving home provided by Warren and Mary Elizabeth Doud Packard. The two first-born boys, William Doud and James Ward Packard, would remain citizens of Warren, Ohio for their entire lives. They would also carry the family's dynamism and entrepreneurial spirit into the Age of Electricity, creating several businesses that would leave their mark on industrial America for over a century. Their companies would provide excellent products to the market, as well as a comfortable income and standard of living for untold tens of thousands of employees and their families in the decades following their start. The automobile which bore their name would carry a prestige far outliving its founders.

The three daughters next born to Warren and Mary Packard – Alaska, Carlotta and Olive – would all leave Warren in adulthood, each traveling in her own interesting path through life. Only two offspring of this generation of Packard children would reach maturity.

Warren Packard II was the child of William Doud and Annie Storer Packard. He was born in Warren, Ohio. His adult life took him first to Cleveland then to Detroit until his tragic death in 1929.

Henry Packard White was the only child of Carl and Olive Packard White, born in Cleveland in 1909. He was a successful businessman, but was not directly involved with the Packard family in Warren.

The following will therefore focus on the lives of Warren Packard and his five adult children, two generations from Warren, Ohio that contributed so much to their hometown and to America.

Stories about the Packards have been told many times throughout the years. Almost all of them have been related to the fine automobile that bears the Packard name. But the Packard family story is about much more than automobiles. It is of a close family of accomplishment, tragedy, business success, affluence and much more.

The story that follows is divided into two parts. Part 1 contains chapters that chronicle the individual lives of the Packards of Warren. These are presented to provide a human face to each of them and to illustrate how the family interacted and worked together. Part 2 emphasizes illustrations and photographs of places, vocations and avocations familiar to the Packard family during their lifetime. While these include descriptions, the images themselves are intended to provide a stronger insight into the world that was theirs. Many of these are previously unpublished.

There is no claim that this story is complete. It is only hoped that the reader will have a better understanding of the Packard family of Warren, Ohio. Perhaps it will motivate some to delve deeper into the lives of these remarkable people, beyond the well-chronicled auto pioneering days.

The following pages also do not highlight or chronicle the lives of other members of the Packard family, some who also lived in Warren or who contributed to the legacy of the Packards in the Western Reserve. Brothers, uncles, close or distant cousins-there were many other Packards that were involved with the subjects of this story. The spouses of the Packards were also very important in the fabric of their lives. They should be the subject of future chroniclers.

The Packard Family of Warren, Ohio

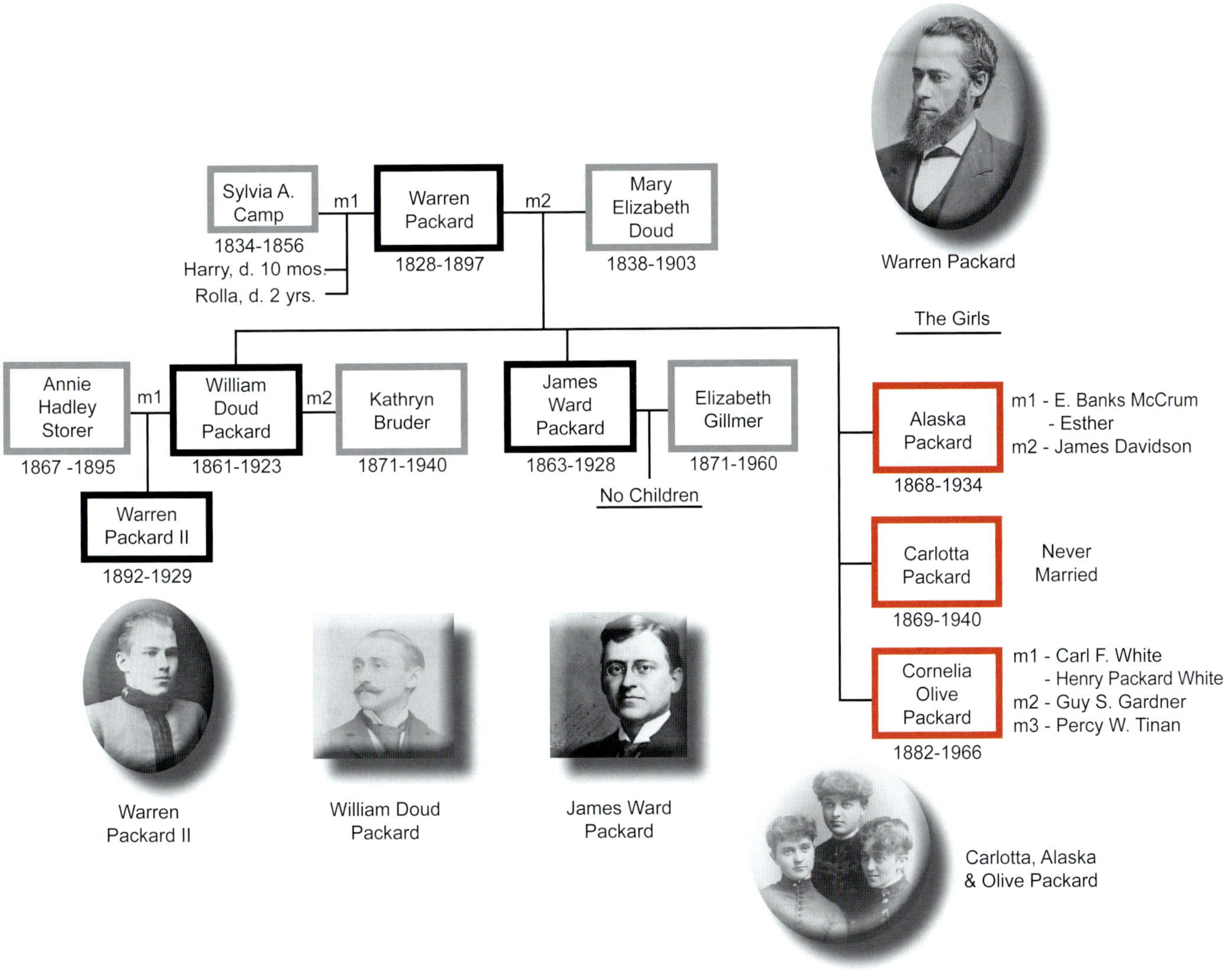

Chapter I

Ipswich to the Western Reserve

The Flat Earth Society had more or less gone into hiding by the beginning of the 17th Century. Ferdinand Magellan's navigator, Juan Sebastian Eleano, had succeeded in becoming the first to circumnavigate the globe by 1522, and Englishman Sir Francis Drake repeated the feat later in the same century. Cartographer Amerigo Vespucci's name soon became permanently attached to the two continents of the New World.

All the maritime powers of Europe hastened to establish colonial rule throughout the New World. Perhaps the most exuberant display of colonialism was Spain's design of coins produced by their American mints. Silver Reales illustrated allegorical Pillars of Hercules, with the Atlantic Ocean ahead and the Latin phrase "Plus Ultra" ("More Beyond") added.

This coinage created vast wealth for Spain, and both Europe and the Americas traded freely with it. Indeed, the Spanish colonial "Ocho Reales" (8 Reales) coin became the later basis for the American silver dollar. Even today, "2 bits"-originally referring to 2 Reales- defines our quarter dollar coin.

The Spaniards were first to colonize the New World. During the 16th Century major enclaves had been settled in Central America, Florida, and the Caribbean. By Papal Edict, the Portuguese were able to add Brasil to their holdings. Even the Dutch created New Amsterdam (New York) in the 1600's. Some French enclaves were established in the Caribbean and on the South American coast.

The North American continent, from the Central Atlantic to the Arctic Circle, was coveted by both the French and the British crowns. As a reflection of their almost continuous state of war in Europe, the matter of French or British dominance from the Atlantic to the Mississippi River in the west would not be decided until the mid-18th century.

The French path to colonization centered around the establishment of Quebec on the St. Lawrence River then a forward push into the North American interior via the Great Lakes.

Alternatively, the British would gravitate to coastal towns, later pushing west as new lands and opportunities arose. The first significant attempts at colonization by the British would be at Jamestown, Virginia in 1607 and Plymouth, Massachusetts in 1620. Settlers began streaming to the New World for a variety of reasons: escape from religious or political persecution, freedom of opportunity, or just plain adventure. The trickle would become a torrent. By the mid-1630s, British ships loaded with passengers bound for the New World were no longer a novelty.

And so it was that the good ship "Diligent" set sail from Ipswich (Suffolk, England) in June of 1638. The Diligent arrived in Boston Harbor on August 10, 1638 and discharged its passengers for settlement in the New World. Among those arrivals were one Samuel Packard, his wife, Elizabeth, and their first-born child, Mary.

Samuel Packard was a direct forebear of the Packard family of Warren, Ohio. Some of Samuel's records in both the Old and the New World are confusing. However, genealogical research by Packard descendants since the mid-19th century have created a plausible and well documented path of his life.

Samuel was born near Wymondham, Suffolk (Norfolk?)–some say Windham–in 1612. The third son of George and Mary Wyther Packard, Samuel was baptized on September 17, 1612 at Stonham Aspel (or Aspall), Suffolk. He married Elizabeth (Washburn?) and together they had 14 children between 1637 and 1657. All but the first child were born in America.

Upon arriving in Boston Harbor the Packards immediately removed to Hingham, located on the south shore of the harbor. That same year Samuel was given a land grant within Hingham where they lived until at least 1652. Hingham had been incorporated in September 1635, and the first settlers were believed to have arrived around 1633. By the arrival of the Diligent, 133 new citizens were added to the town's rolls.

Around 1654 the family moved to Weymouth, an inland town about 5 miles southwest of Hingham. They again moved to Bridgewater in 1662 where Samuel lived until his death in July 1684. During his life in the New World he had been involved in many community service positions including selectman, constable, tax collector and surveyor. In 1670 Samuel was granted a license to operate a tavern, a vocation he followed until his death.

Some confusion has surrounded Samuel's surname. It has been variously written as Packer, Pecker, Peckerd, Peckard and Parker. Although a respected member of his community, Samuel always signed documents with a mark, suggesting that he could not write.

Genealogical research of the Packard family descended from Samuel began in earnest by the mid-19th century. After 200 years in the New World the family had increased geometrically. Although still numerous in Massachusetts, Packards had pushed into most inhabited regions of the country. They had also helped occupy and settle the wilderness regions of western Pennsylvania and eastern Ohio. These Ohio lands were known as the Western Reserve.

In 1662 the Connecticut Colony had been granted a charter by the English King Charles II, recognizing their right to all lands "sea-to-sea" between the 41st and 42nd (+2 minutes) parallels. This was soon interrupted by establishment of the Commonwealth of Pennsylvania within those bounds. Yet Connecticut still claimed the lands that lay to the west of Pennsylvania. However, after the Revolutionary War Connecticut ceded to the federal government all its western land claims in exchange for federal assumption of the state's war debts and obligations.....except for 3.37 million acres directly west of the Pennsylvania line. This retained land was originally called "New Connecticut," soon discarded in favor of "Western Reserve."

By 1796 the State of Connecticut found it desirable to sell off the Western Reserve, and in 1803 it became part of the new State of Ohio. Western Reserve towns of Youngstown (1769), Warren (1798), Hudson and Ravenna (1799) became part of our 17th state. The "Western Reserve" moniker still exists today in many descriptions and businesses from Cleveland to the Pennsylvania border.

Samuel's arrival in the New World (1638) was celebrated by a large gathering of the Packard clan in August of 1888 in Brockton, Massachusetts. The Packard Memorial Association published an impressive booklet commemorating the gathering, "Celebration of the Two Hundred and Fiftieth Anniversary of the Landing of Samuel Packard." Filled with a brief history of their ancestor Samuel and speeches honoring the gathering, the booklet also contained a listing of over 500 Packard descendants attending. There were Packard representatives from Maine to California but none from Western Penn-

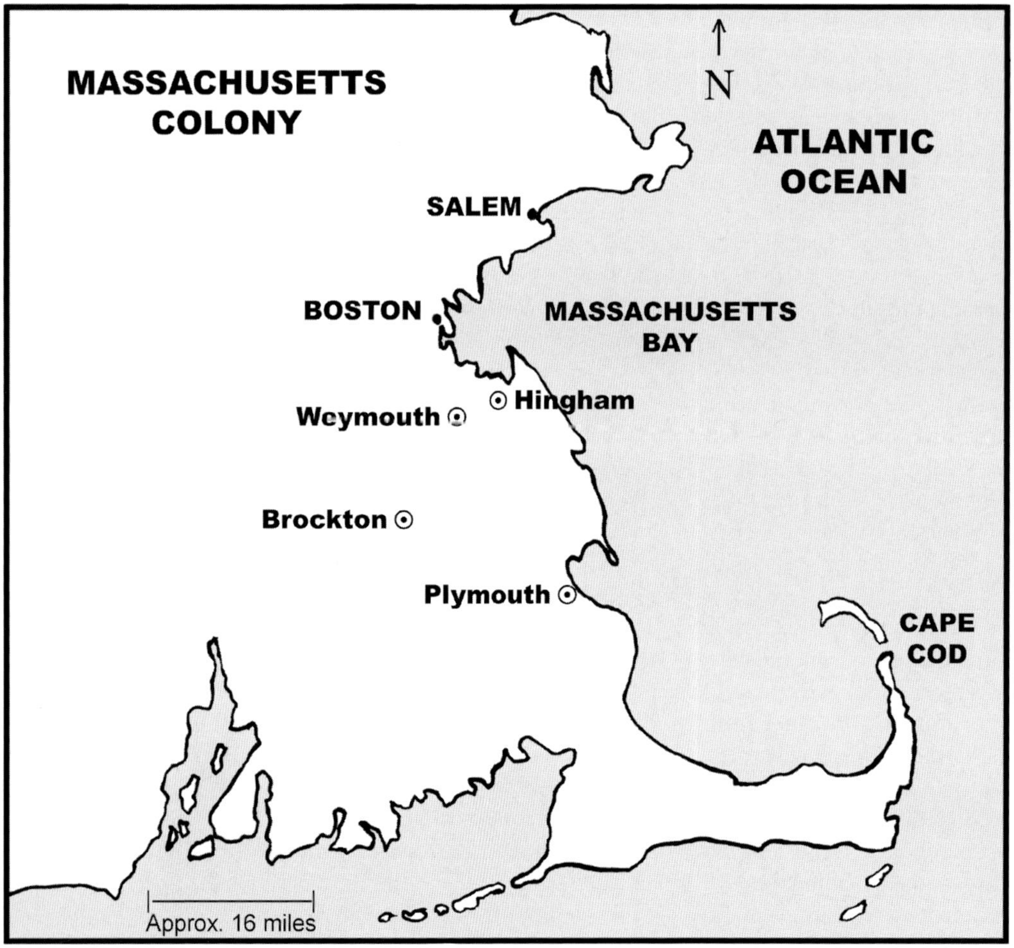

The New World for Samuel Packard

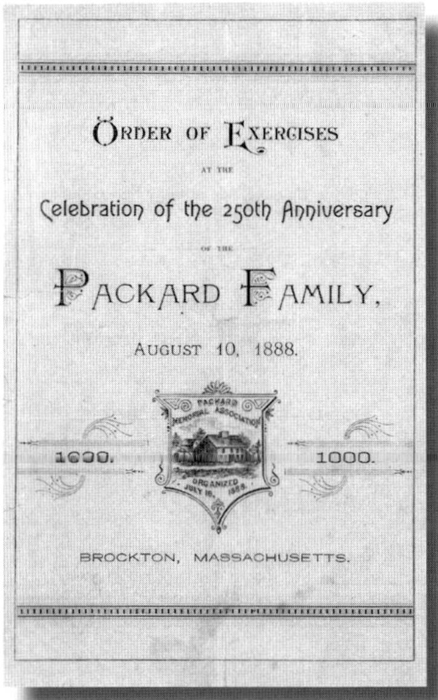

Folder outlining Packard Reunion Activities, August 10, 1888

sylvania and the Western Reserve. The booklet mentioned that almost 2000 families of Samuel's descendants had been identified.

By-laws were established at this meeting for the perpetuation of the Packard Memorial Association, and an internal group was organized to promote further identity and preservation of the Packard family genealogy. DeWitt Clinton Packard of Brockton, Massachusetts was elected president of the association. There were 26 vice-presidents representing various regions of America who were also elected. Many of these were not attending the Brockton gathering, including John Randolph Packard of Greenville, Pennsylvania. John was the brother of Warren Packard and had established a hardware business in Greenville with his uncle, Daniel Berry Packard. He would move to Warren, Ohio in 1864 and enter business with his brother Warren. Both of them would be involved with the Greenville business and John would later return to live in Greenville.

The Packard family had not arrived in the Western Reserve until after Ohio attained statehood. Thomas Packard (1778-1851) settled in Washington County, Pennsylvania and son William (1803-1877) was the first of the twelve children born to them. William married Julia Anne Leach of New Jersey in June 1826. One of the twelve children born to them was Warren Packard, the father of William Doud and James Ward Packard.

William was the first Packard to settle on the lands described as the Western Reserve. He migrated to the Austintown-Lordstown area in 1825 and soon established himself as an active and responsible member of the community. Unsuccessful in his run for Ohio State Senator, he became Postmaster of Lordstown in 1835.

The California Gold Rush of 1849 forever changed the Packard family. Although several of the older children had attained maturity, Julia still had the younger children in her care. Warren Packard had left their Lordstown home at age 18 in 1846 to find his future in Warren, Ohio.

But gold fever had taken control of William. He left his family, and with three companions (Daniel Jagger, James Abell and Robert Quigley) left for the California gold fields in the summer of 1849 to seek his fortune. West of Salt Lake City two of the group died of cholera and were buried along the trail. William's trek west had consumed six months, and his arrival in Sacramento was less than enthusiastic. He never found gold and spent several years struggling to survive.

William ultimately moved to the foothills of Greenhorn Mountain in Kern County (California) where he established a small ranch raising Angora goats. He pursued this lonely life until shortly before his death.

Much lore has surfaced regarding the California life of William Packard. He has been variously described as a Justice of the

1826 Map of the Western Reserve

Peace and a respected judge in Kern County (Bakersfield). This description more logically belongs to his brother, Newton Reed Packard (1823-1900). Newton first arrived in Kern County in 1874 and was indeed a Justice of the Peace and respected member of the community there. He was Kern County Clerk well into the 1890's. This was certainly in contrast to the isolated life of his brother.

Communication between William and his family in the Western Reserve was non-existent between 1849 and April of 1865. Although letters had been written between California and Ohio, none had ever been delivered to the addressee. The family in Ohio assumed that William had died, and William could not understand why his letters never deserved a reply from across the continent. In his solitude he wrote one last time early in 1865 to his sons John, Warren, Frank, and Andrew Packard. The letter was received by Frank at the Warren, Ohio Post Office on April 1, 1865. At first Frank thought that this was an April Fool's joke. But comparison with William's pre-1849 writings soon convinced the brothers that their father was still alive!

With proper addresses established, communication between father and family began anew.

In 1869 William's son-in-law and daughter, Jerome and Ellen Packard Campbell, with their daughters Gertrude and Renee, traveled by stagecoach and transcontinental railroad to California for an emotional reunion. The Golden Spike had finished the joining of the Central Pacific and Union Pacific Railroads at Promontory Point, Utah-near Salt Lake City-on May 10, 1869. This event linked both sides of the American continent, and dramatically reduced the time required to travel from coast to coast. Jerome and Ellen were among the first to travel to the west by rail.

Julia Leach Packard (Mrs. William Packard, Grandmother of William Doud & James Ward Packard.)

Five years later, in 1874, sons Warren, John, Frank, and Andrew again took the railroad west. They surprised their father at his Greenhorn Mountain ranch. For several hours William had no idea who his Eastern visitors were.....when they finally divulged their true identity the reunion became loving and emotional. The boys stayed with their father for several weeks and William considered returning to Ohio and his family. By 1877 he had finally settled most of his affairs and was preparing to return to the home and family that he had left behind 28 years before. But William contracted a fever and died on December 11, 1877. He was buried in his adopted California.

William's widow Julia lived until December 1891. Her sons, Warren and John, had built a small house for her on Monroe Street in Warren, where she spent the last chapter of her life. Eighty five years old when she died, Julia was the last of the Ohio Packard clan who could remember the pioneering days in the old Western Reserve.

The Packard Family from Western Pennsylvania and Eastern Ohio

*Thomas Packard**

1778-1851

- William Packard* 1803-1877 — Julia Anne Leach* 1806-1891
  - Angelina Packard Weisell*
  - Warren Packard* 1828-1897
  - Nancy A. Packard
  - Calvin Packard/Nelson Packard
  - Andrew Jackson Packard*
  - John Randolph Packard*
  - Ellen D. Packard Campbell*
  - Benjamin Franklin Packard*
  - Elias Packard
  - Milton A. Packard
  - Mary L. Packard
- Garrison B. Packard
- John A. Packard
- Thomas A. Packard
- Rezin Berry Packard
- Anna Maria Packard Christman
- Daniel Berry Packard*
- Loverayn Packard
- Newton Reed Packard* 1823-1900
- Jasper Packard
- Andrew Packard
- Henry Packard

**Family members are mentioned throughout this Packard story.*

Chapter 2

A Busy Life — Warren Packard

Warren Packard was the first of Will and Ward's direct line to be born in the Western Reserve. The second child of William and Julia Packard, Warren was born on June 1, 1828 at Austintown, then in Mahoning County.

With daughters Angelina and Nancy and son Warren, the William Packard family had moved to Lordstown in 1834. The Packard children included four girls and eight boys ranging in age from 2 to 22 by 1849, when father William left for the California gold fields. Julia was now on her own to raise this large family.

The given names of the children in the Packard family reveal to a large extent the respect that William fostered for Americans he admired. Andrew Jackson Packard, John Randolph Packard and Benjamin Franklin Packard all were known in later years as A.J., John R., and Frank or B.F. Daughter Nancy Ann was probably named for her paternal grandmother Nancy A. Berry Packard. Warren was likely named for Moses Warren, the pioneer surveyor of the town of Warren, Ohio. The town itself was founded in 1798 by Ephraim Quinby on land he purchased from the Connecticut Land Company. Warren became the county seat of Trumbull County in 1801.

Warren Packard's children in the next generation would continue to be named for family, friends, and, in one case, an historical event.

Warren Packard's business life was active and successful with all the chaotic elements that normally accompany dynamic people. He was intelligent, honest and compassionate, always carried himself exceptionally well, and was willing to take substantial risks for profit in business. He was not afraid to try new directions. During the course of his career Warren joined with many different business partners in various enterprises. It was a testament to his success and fairness to these partners that several of them were later active participants in Will and Ward's businesses.

When Warren was eighteen years old he walked from Lordstown to Warren, Ohio with all of his worldly possessions on his back. His father William would remain at home for two more years before leaving for California. This trek to Warren would herald the beginning of Warren Packard's new life and expansive business career.

The town of Warren had approximately 1,600 citizens when Warren Packard arrived in 1846. There were at that time five churches, twenty-odd stores, one bank, a woolen factory and two flour mills in town. The vibrancy and opportunity of this growing community were major attractions for the young Packard.

Warren's older sister Angelina had recently married Eli Weisell, a cooper by trade living in Warren. Through his recommendation young Packard secured boarding in Warren in the home of Milton Graham, who owned the local hardware store. He had arrived with nothing more than the clothes on his back and very few worldly possessions. It would have been difficult then to foresee the meteoric business success and personal triumphs and tragedies he would experience in the years ahead.

Young Warren couldn't pay the Grahams with hard cash for his keep. Instead, he was expected to "lighten the load" of the household by taking on the responsibility for certain chores. These included tending the family's cows and team of horses and chopping firewood – a continuing chore from spring until the onset of the next winter.

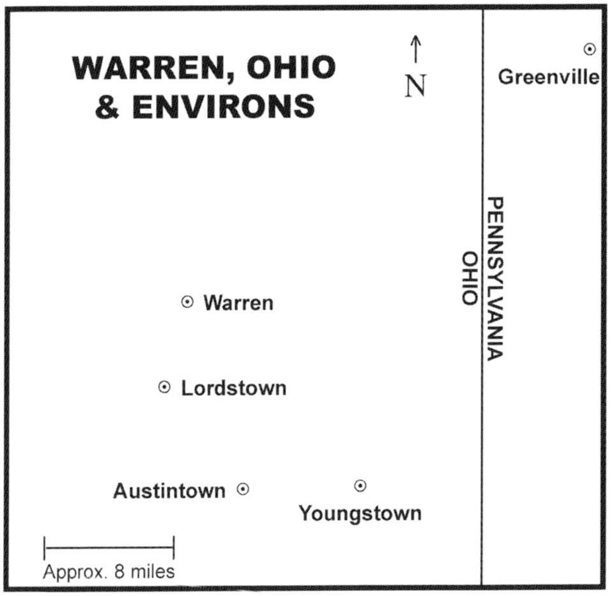

Warren Packard's World – The Early Years

There was also a need to remain on duty at the hardware store while Mr. Graham and his sons went home for lunch. On Saturdays young Warren was assigned the task of driving the Graham team and wagon to Niles and Youngstown to purchase new inventory for the Graham Hardware store. Most of these purchases were of iron products such as nails and hinges, but many other necessities or small luxuries of 19th century life would also come back to the store.

During the first year of his residency with the Graham family, Warren attended school for penmanship, ciphering and English.

For the second year of his stay with the family Warren was expected to continue with the same responsibilities as before in exchange for his room and board. Now a salary of $100 a year was added.

By 1851 Warren Packard was the sole owner of the Graham hardware business. Milton Graham had several sons, and the reason for their departure from the business is not known. Now Warren Packard would begin his mercurial rise in the world of business. From this moment on his entrepreneurial influence and success would unfold in many directions.

Warren also took some time at this juncture to court the daughter of local hotel proprietor Alanson Camp. Warren and Sylvia were married in Warren on September 21, 1852.

This marriage was marked by tragedy several times over within a few short years. Their first son Harry was born early in 1855. The boy died at age ten months. Their second son Rolla was born in the fall of 1856. He was named in honor of one of Warren's friends and future business partners, Rolla Barnum. His mother Sylvia died of complications a few weeks after Rolla's birth, on December 4, 1856. Tragically, Rolla also died at the young age of two in 1858. Warren Packard was now a widower without a wife or children at age 30.

In 1855 Warren Packard acquired a burial plot in Oakwood Cemetery to provide a final resting place for his family. Oakwood had been organized and opened in 1849. The original Packard plot includes Lot 106 and the west ½ of Lot 107, in Section O.P. (original part of the cemetery). The plot was of sufficient size to accommodate ten burials and today holds the mortal remains of ten Packards from four generations. One additional burial of cremains was made in 1998 of Warren Packard's great granddaughter. Visitors to Oakwood today can easily locate this burial plot by the large monument with the family name in large traditional Packard script.

At about the time of Sylvia's death, Warren was beginning the expansion of his hardware enterprises. His brother John R. and uncle Daniel B. Packard had formed a hardware business in Greenville, Pennsylvania called Packard & Co. in 1854. Warren invested in this as a partner and the business was incorporated in 1892 as the Packard Hardware Co. After Warren's death in 1897, John R. became president. Will Packard, as executor of his father's estate, spent considerable time attempting to preserve, identify and liquidate Warren's assets in the Greenville business.

Warren Packard, Entrepreneur and Merchant

By 1860 Warren had again courted a young lady from Warren, Ohio–Mary Elizabeth Doud, daughter of William C. and Ann Paltzgroff Doud. They were married on November 20, 1860 and would become the parents of five children who would live to maturity, including Will and Ward.

It was about this time that Warren would partner with another of his brothers, A.J., in the hardware business in Youngstown. This business was also very successful until 1873 when a fire completely destroyed the assets of W. & A.J. Packard Hardware Co. of Youngstown.

Another investment in the early 1860's was a partnership with Rolla Barnum. Packard & Barnum's Forge & Rolling Mill became a large enterprise southeast of the corner of Pine and South Streets, producing bar iron, plate and nails. The capital investment in this business was substantial. By the early 1870's, a declining market for iron products plus the fire at the Youngstown hardware business resulted in a loss of $200,000 for Warren Packard – a huge sum in those days.

Beginning in the early 1860's, Warren had also expanded his portfolio to include investments in the lumber business. With S.L. Abell and Harmon Austin he operated a sawmill just west of Warren, Ohio's town limits on the line of the C & M Railroad. This fortunate entry into lumber would prove to be a major contributor to Warren Packard's fortune, especially after 1862 and until the early 1890's. Tracts of lumber in Western Pennsylvania, West Virginia and Kentucky would ultimately be secured by Warren. Sawmills were set up on site to process shingles for housing as well as boards for plank roads. Even more lucrative was the supply of railroad ties and bridge materials to the railroads at a time when various lines were being laid out and developed by the fast-growing railroad industry. One of the major customers of Warren Packard was the Atlantic & Great Western Railway, later absorbed as a major part of the Erie Line.

It was a most convenient coincidence that passenger trains scheduled on the A & GW RR connected Warren, Ohio and Lakewood, New York, located near Jamestown on Lake Chautauqua in the western part of the Finger Lakes region. Warren Packard would next mix business with pleasure on the shores of Chautauqua.

Prior to the disastrous fire at Youngstown and the declining income of the iron business, Warren did make a significant commitment that reflected his new-found wealth. He embarked on an extensive Grand Tour of Europe in 1867. In those days such an undertaking was a major financial and time-consuming event. Will and Ward were only six and four at that time. It isn't known if the entire Warren Packard family made this trip together. Before the turn of the century, son Will had repeated the feat twice again.

Even after the fire and losses at Packard & Barnum, it was evident that Warren Packard's fortune was still substantial.... Diversification into lumber and other investments in ventures such as the Austin Flagstone Co. had proven quite lucrative.

Warren Packard In Later Life

In 1870 Warren had acquired very desirable property on High Street which ran from the Opera House block to Mahoning Avenue facing the courthouse square. By 1874 he had approved construction of a large new 3-story mansion of French Mansard design which was ready for occupancy during 1876. The family lived here until 1902. The house and adjacent carriage house were built of the finest workmanship and materials available. The wide staircases, heavy banisters and massive wooden doors were all of solid walnut, much of it hand carved. Accommodations were also made in the house for the necessary servants. After Mary Doud Packard moved to the Packard Apartments with daughters Carlotta and Olive in 1902, the mansion became occupied by Harriet Taylor Upton's National Suffrage Movement and then Hall's Music Store. It subsequently became a restaurant for a short period of time and was then purchased by the Elks Lodge. It was torn down in 1963 to make way for an addition to the YMCA.

At about the same time work was beginning on the Packard mansion in 1874, Warren with his brothers John R., A.J., and B.F., journeyed to Kern County, California to confront and visit their father William. The way had been paved in 1869 by their sister, Ellen Packard Campbell, her husband and their children. This would be the last time any of the Packard children would see their father.

By 1874, Warren Packard and his brother John R. had also further diversified their investments, this time in a totally new direction. They invested in a resort hotel on Lake Chautauqua named "Lakeview House". Warren additionally acquired twenty-five acres of land adjacent to the hotel and proceeded to build a $3000 "cottage" near the hotel as his vacation retreat. This land would subsequently become the "Lakeview Trust" of the new town of Lakewood. The Lakeview House was razed in 1889 and replaced by the Sterlingworth Hotel. It and the neighboring Kent House Hotel were sold to the Lakewood Hotel & Land Co. in 1896. The Sterlingworth was renamed The Waldmere, becoming an annex to the Kent House. It was destroyed by fire in 1903 and never rebuilt.

Warren Packard, his wife and children would all enjoy the Lakewood setting as their vacation home. Both Will and Ward would build large mansions here in the 2nd decade of the 20th century.

Warren Packard died on July 28, 1897. He was 69 years old. His son Will was executor of his estate. For the next fifteen years he was deeply involved in liquidating or reorganizing his father's many businesses. It was fitting of Warren Packard that he would write his autobiography which he did shortly before his death. His story was transcribed and finalized by his son Will, with copies distributed to the family. It was telling that Warren titled his life story, "A Busy Life," and that the pages were filled with an outline of his business career. Only four sentences at the end contained any description of his family and their lives together.

Mary Elizabeth Doud Packard died of a stroke on October 9, 1903. This was the day before the Packard Motor Car Company founded by her sons moved to a new beginning in Detroit. She was 64 years old. She was buried in the Paltzgroff family plot with her mother's family in Lordstown.

Mary Doud Packard in the 1890's.

Chapter 3

The First Son — William Doud

The guns aimed at Fort Sumter in Charleston Harbor erupted on April 12, 1861 signaling the start of a long and bloody American Civil War. Mary Elizabeth Doud Packard was by then aware of her pregnancy. Her first-born child, a son named William Doud Packard, was born on November 3 later that year.

Named for his maternal grandfather, he was known by family and friends throughout his life as Will. Some acquaintances, particularly in business, referred to him as W.D. The more familiar "Will" was the name most recognized in a household that attached special monikers to all but one of the children.

Warren was 33 years old when Will was born. The family was beginning to enjoy the great financial success that Warren's hard work and entrepreneurship had brought them. They still lived, at the time of Will's birth, in a rented house on the northwest corner of Elm and East Market Streets in Warren. Second son Ward would also be born in this house almost two years later.

Mary was 22 years of age when Will was born. Her five children would arrive between 1861 and 1882-a span of 21 years. All would be born at home. The last child, Cornelia Olive, did not round out the roster of Packard children until thirteen years after the last previous birth of Carlotta. Warren was 54 years old when Olive arrived.

Six hundred thousand (600,000) Americans died in the Civil War. Most families North and South were deeply affected in various ways by the conflict that had dragged on for four long years. Both volunteers and conscripts had begun to swell the ranks of the opposing armies early on. Federal laws were enacted and continued throughout the conflict that allowed men who were subject to the draft to provide a substitute for military duty upon payment of a $300 bounty for the substitute conscript.

No records have been found to date of military service by Warren Packard or any of his brothers. It is a fair assumption that they paid the bounties.

Will had all the benefits of a stable, loving and affluent home life as he grew to maturity. The Packard children all appear to have been very close and all except Ward were socially very active and involved. Until the time of their marriages, family activities were the centerpiece of their lives individually and collectively. In periods of stress the entire Packard family could be counted on to "circle the wagons" and protect their own.

Each of the children exhibited characteristics that defined them throughout their lives. Will thrived on the business of business. Bookkeeping, organization, contractual development and especially salesmanship and business relationships defined his career. These talents were to afford a very successful symbiotic relationship with younger brother Ward that would propel them and their businesses to the first rank of American industry for several decades beginning in the 1890's.

None of this was yet apparent as Will attended public schools in Warren. He then traveled to Columbus in 1879 at age 18 to attend the Ohio Agricultural and Mechanical College, now known as Ohio State University. In his time at the school he passed Elementary Physics and Mechanical Drawing. He was given conditional passes for Elementary Chemistry and Mechanical Laboratory. Clearly a technical curriculum was not suited to Will's talent or interests. He returned to Warren after two terms and went to work for his father. As was the case for all the Packard children who attended college, father Warren paid Will's tuition and living expenses for the time spent in Columbus. It was another matter after his return.

Warren taught all of his children to be individually responsible adults. With the exception of Will's younger sister Carlotta, all of the Packard children were expected to support themselves through marriage and also hard work. There was no "free lunch". The children were even required to pay room and board if they were inclined to move back into the large family mansion on High Street. Some of Will's diaries illustrate in great detail the expenses of living with the family after the death of his first wife.

During the decade of the 1880's Will spent most of his time working and learning in his father's various business enterprises. Until the time of his marriage in 1891 he lived in the High Street mansion overlooking Courthouse Square built by his father. He was the bookkeeper and accountant for the hardware businesses, the iron forge and rolling mill off South Street, and for the Lakeview Hotel in Lakewood, New York. He even became proficient in telegraphy, a skill he put to use in both Warren and Lakewood.

There was a brief time during 1887 when Will had decided to work in the new and exciting electrical industry. He went to New York City and spent a few months with the Thomson-Houston Company, a major producer of electrical transformers, con-

Will at the time of his Grand Tour of Europe, 1889

trol equipment and light bulbs. They had purchased the Sawyer-Man Company in 1886 and employed both Will and brother Ward at this time. Their exposure to Sawyer-Man/Thomson-Houston products and markets would have major significance in the creation of several Packard electrical manufacturing companies in the last decade of the 19th century.

Will did not enjoy the reality of living in New York City and returned to Warren after a brief period of time. He never deserted his roots in Warren or his later summer home near Lakewood again. His brother Ward permanently returned to his hometown during 1890 as well, after spending six years with Sawyer-Man and Thomson-Houston in New York City.

After spending most of the decade of the 1880's immersed in his father's businesses, the daily ritual and tempo of Will's life was to change dramatically. His personal actions and outside influences on his life were to lead to a relatively chaotic existence for the next 15 years.

In 1889 Will embarked on a Grand Tour of Europe much as his father had done back in 1867. With departure on September 16 aboard the "SS Furnessia" bound for Glasgow, his itinerary began and ended in Britain. This included overland travel through France, the Italian peninsula, Germany and the Low Countries. He arrived back in New York aboard the "City of Paris" on December 17.

His visit to Paris coincided with the Universal Exposition (World's Fair) of 1889, which celebrated the 100th anniversary of the French Revolution. The entrance arch for the Exposition was designed by Gustave Eiffel and is commonly known as the Eiffel Tower, today one of the best-known monuments on the globe. At the time of its construction the tower was the tallest man-made structure in the world at 986 feet, a record which stood until the Chrysler Building was built in New York City in 1930.

But the tower's feature that most excited Will was the brilliant electrification that acted as a nightly beacon to the Left Bank of the Seine River. He recognized from this the great transformational power that the Age of Electricity would bring to the world. Later, when he attended the Columbian Exposition (1893 World's Fair) in Chicago, the incandescent lighting was so brilliant that the Exposition grounds were dubbed the White City. The New York & Ohio Company, for which Will was secretary and treasurer, was a popular major exhibitor at the Exposition.

After the Grand Tour, it was time to create a Packard business to supply the demands of this new and exciting Electrical Age. The opportunities appeared limitless.

Will and Ward had for several years analyzed the electrical business and decided that they could successfully produce and supply electrical equipment and light bulbs just as well as any of the other producers. From the technical point of view, there were two primary areas of conflict in electrification of cities that were playing out during the late 19th century. First was the question of direct current (DC) versus alternating current (AC) for major electrification systems and grids. Thomas Edison had been a proponent of DC current (early supported by General Electric), while Nicola Tesla promoted AC current (supported by Westinghouse). Ultimately, the technical benefits of AC current supply won the day. The second question was with regard to light bulbs-incandescent versus arc lights. Both types have been proven desirable in specific applications. Will and Ward correctly emphasized AC equipment for their major new systems product line. For a long period of time they produced both incandescent and arc lamps for the market.

So with the business expertise of Will and the technical expertise of Ward, the two brothers created in 1890 the Packard Electric Company of Warren, Ohio. Ward was president and Will was secretary/treasurer. Their initial local stock offering was not adequately subscribed. It was evident that more capital was required. A new subscription by investors from Ward's New York contacts was successfully made and a parallel company, The New York & Ohio Company, was incorporated in January 1891. Both companies worked closely together for many years. Will was again secretary/treasurer.

Events were now moving rapidly in Will's life. After the creation and incorporation of both Packard Electric and the New York & Ohio Companies, the next step would be to organize the factory for production, and solicit business for their products. Ward was given responsibility for the former and Will hit the road for the latter. He would spend considerable time over the

Probably Annie Storer Packard around the time of her marriage to Will in 1891

next fifteen years promoting the product in many cities and towns east of the Mississippi. Representation in the west was more often initiated by prospective dealers and distributors.

Just as urgent for Will during 1890 and early 1891 was the courtship of a pretty and personable young lady from New England named Annie Hadley Storer. Annie had first come to Will's attention during her visit in Warren with an old school friend, Sally Woods, now Mrs. Harmon Austin, daughter-in-law of one of Warren Packard's business associates. Born in 1867 in West Roxbury, Massachusetts, Annie and Will were married in June 1891 at Middlesex, Connecticut. The newlyweds returned to Warren and took up residence at 7 North Elm Street.

A son named for his grandfather, Warren Packard II, was born in 1892. Tragedy would soon strike. In June 1895, after lingering for several weeks, Annie succumbed to complications from appendix surgery. She left behind a grieving husband and a child not yet three years old. Annie was the fourth Packard buried in the family plot in Oakwood Cemetery.

Will and young Warren II moved back to the Packard mansion on High Street in January 1897 where they would live until the family moved to the new Packard Apartments on Park Avenue in 1902. Warren Sr. died in July 1897 at age 69 and was the fifth Packard to be buried in the family plot that he himself had purchased forty-two years earlier.

Will paid room and board for both himself and Warren II. His work schedule remained intense and other family members were enlisted to handle much of Warren II's care. Carlotta, Will's younger sister, was especially involved in raising the boy during these early formative years.

Still mourning the loss of his young wife, Will had continued planning for his second European visit during 1895. The purpose of this visit was to observe European advances in electrical equipment technology. He also acquired and arranged shipment for a new DeDion-Bouton Motorette tricycle for Ward. This was one of the first successful gasoline engine-powered vehicles in Europe. It marked the beginning of a dedicated interest in horseless carriages by the Packard brothers.

In these times Will also belonged to several fraternal and service organizations including the Masonic Order and the International Concatenated Order of Hoo-Hoo, Incorporated. The latter organization consists of members of the forest products industry and still has chapters in several countries around the world, including the United States. Their chartered purpose is to foster the health, happiness and long life of members. Will would attend evening Hoo-Hoo meetings in various large cities when he would be held over there for several days.

By late 1899 the Packard brothers were prepared to test their first automobile, which successfully completed its inaugural run on November 6. Will had joined his brother and George L. Weiss of Cleveland in a partnership that opened the development of their automobile venture. In September 1900 they dissolved the Packard & Weiss partnership and incorporated that business as the Ohio Automobile Company. Will was again secretary/treasurer. A year later the company was re-incorporated as the Packard Motor Car Company, a respected name and leader in the automotive industry for over fifty years.

In October 1903, when the Packard Motor Car Company was moved to Detroit, Will resigned as a director of the company while retaining his significant stock holdings. His investments in this company as well as in Packard Electric and the New York and Ohio Company would translate into a substantial fortune in the years to come.

Tragedy had again struck in that month of October, as Mary Elizabeth Doud Packard suffered a severe stroke and died on October 9. It was the day before the Packard Motor Car Company officially closed down operations in Warren and reopened in Detroit. Mary Doud Packard was buried in the Paltzgroff family plot (her mother's family) in Lordstown, Ohio.

During the years since formation of the Packard automobile business, Will had continued to promote the electrical businesses of Packard Electric and the New York & Ohio Company. In 1904 the latter business became affiliated with the National Electric Lamp Association (NELA) with its primary product evolving as the incandescent light bulb. In 1911 the company was sold to General Electric and Will continued only as a stockholder. On the Packard Electric side of the business, this company had pioneered many products for the new and rapidly expanding automobile industry, including wiring harnesses and specialized connectors and wiring materials. The company was reorganized with new investors and management in 1916 and was subsequently acquired as a division of General Motors Corporation in 1932.

After again living for five years at the Packard mansion on High Street, Will, along with the rest of the family, moved in January of 1902 into the luxurious new Packard Apartments on North Park Avenue. He had for some time taken many of his meals at the Park Hotel on Warren's Courthouse Square where a young lady named Kathryn Bruder was the head waiter. Within a few days of moving into the Packard Apartments, Will had hired Kitty as his housekeeper at $25 a month.

The housekeeping arrangement continued and Will, capitalizing on his substantial business success, decided to build a large new home. River Court, on Mahoning Avenue, was built in 1905. Will and Kitty Bruder were married the next year at Ward's Lakewood cottage and the newlyweds settled in at River Court.

Will's business activities were stepping away from the chaotic pace he had established over fifteen years before. Although he did participate as a director in Ward's short-lived Packard/Liberty car agency in Buffalo beginning in 1916, he was now no longer the driving force in the businesses he had helped create.

Instead, he undertook the development of a park for the city of Warren that he himself would give to the city. He would also build two more substantial homes-one in Warren and the other near Lakewood.

In 1911 Will acquired 44 acres of attractive land between the Mahoning River and Mahoning Avenue NW in Warren. The land had originally been targeted as a campus for a new state college. When that fell through, Will then conceived the idea for a beautiful park that would include many attractions for the people of Warren and the area. With himself totally involved in its development, it was largely completed by 1915. Its formal dedication, with much pomp and ceremony, took place on July 5, 1915. Under the terms of his Last Will & Testament, funds were also included for the construction of a music hall on the property and the endowment of a local orchestra for the entertainment of Warren residents.

The W. D. Packard Music Hall was finally built in 1955 with funding from Will's estate. To this day the W. D. Packard Band, endowed by Will, performs there.

Immediately after deeding Packard Park to the city of Warren, Will again immersed himself in the construction of a new summer home on Lake Chautauqua, about fifteen miles from the lakeside summer residence of his brother Ward in Lakewood. The beautiful mansion was completed in 1916 and named Packard Manor by Will. It is still today an imposing and well-maintained private residence.

Will's eyesight had been deteriorating for many years. By now, he was essentially blind. Nevertheless, he undertook another major project. This time it was the construction of a new home in Warren. Located across the street close by his home River Court, on the northeast corner of North Avenue and Mahoning Avenue NW, Packard Place was completed in 1920. Today it is a nursing home.

Will died at Packard Place on November 11, 1923, just a few days after his 62nd birthday. His death was due to complications from a viral infection. He was the sixth Packard to be buried in the family plot in Oakwood Cemetery.

Kitty lived on at Packard Place until her death in February 1940. She was then laid to rest as the seventh Packard buried in the family plot in Oakwood Cemetery.

Will, Kitty and Warren II, ca 1920

Chapter 4

The Second Son — James Ward

Mary Doud Packard's second child, a son, was born on November 5, 1863. Abraham Lincoln would deliver his immortal Gettysburg Address in Pennsylvania exactly two weeks later. The new child was named James Ward Packard after a Niles, Ohio business friend of his father, thus continuing the generational Packard practice of choosing meaningful given names for their children. This son would be known as Ward for his entire life. He would be the last Packard born in the rented house on the northwest corner of Elm and East Market Streets.

Ward's brother Will was almost two years older. Together they would later forge entrepreneurial alliances that created a giant American industrial presence which endured for over a century. They both matured during the development of the Electrical Age and its golden opportunities. They also saw the promise of the new-fangled horseless carriage and built a better one. These were exciting times, and the Packard successes were due in large measure to the symbiotic talents of the two brothers.

Ward's early years were typical of many children in the developing upper middle class of the late 19th Century. He attended the public schools in Warren and succeeded with unassuming regularity.

From an early age, Ward didn't fit the mold of contemporary youths. Ward had two distinct characteristics that set him apart.

First was his extreme shyness which later evolved into a reticence that made it difficult to develop close friendships outside of his family. This trait was well identified in an April 1928 letter to Henry Joy from Ward's widow, Elizabeth Gillmer Packard, where she recalled his personal tension in social contacts: "I was always sorry that his inborn shyness made it so hard for him to go to meetings that he finally gave up entirely and resigned from the Packard Motor Car Company in 1915. He always enjoyed the meeting after they were over but he worried himself almost sick whenever he had to go to Detroit. His shyness caused him more suffering than most people realized."

Equally as important to Ward's persona was his inquisitive nature. His mechanical aptitude was apparent at an early age, and he was known to have taken apart such things as door locks, firearms and other small machines from the Packard household. By the age of ten he had dismantled several clocks in the Packard household and successfully reassembled them. He had just wanted to know how they worked.

Later, when Ward's wealth allowed him to indulge in the specification and acquisition of complicated timepieces, his watch collection would be considered as the best in America.

James Ward Packard, about 7 years old

In 1880 this shy but inquisitive young man left Warren to attend Lehigh University in Bethlehem, Pennsylvania. Founded in 1865 by Asa Packer, Lehigh was already a prestigious eastern university with an outstanding Mechanical Engineering program. Many Lehigh alumnae were to become leaders of American commerce and industry. This included Alvan Macauley, class of 1892, long-serving president of the Packard Motor Company.

Ward would later remember his alma mater with substantial gifts which included enabling Lehigh to construct a new engineering building. The James Ward Packard Laboratory of Electrical and Mechanical Engineering was dedicated October 15-17, 1930 and is still in use today. The main entrance hall houses 1899 Packard auto number one as a reminder of Ward's genius. The car had been a gift to Lehigh from the Packard Motor Car Company.

He was still 17 years old when he left Warren for Bethlehem. At the time of his class of 1884 graduation with a Bachelor of Science degree in Mechanical Engineering, Ward was the youngest Lehigh recipient ever to have received it.

The final hurdle for graduation was to submit an approved thesis on a subject germane to the curriculum at Lehigh, exhibiting a working knowledge of that subject. Ward's thesis was titled, "Design of a Dynamo Electrical Machine." The bound original,

James Ward Packard, while a student at Lehigh

including forty handwritten pages and additional drawings of necessary component parts, still exists in the Lehigh University library. It describes an electrical generator designed and sized to illuminate four arc lamps with a total of 8000 candle power. According to Ward's design calculations, such a generator (dynamo) would require a power source of about four horsepower. His thorough understanding of electrical design parameters would serve Ward well in the years to come.

Some notations in Ward's diaries relate to life at Bethlehem. As was ultimately true for all the Packard children, his father Warren paid for the family members' higher education. Ward received $545 from him for the 1882 school year and $707 for 1883, which was a princely sum in those days.

Several of Ward's classmates remembered him as intense, intelligent and very inquisitive. While he had no trouble mastering all of his classes, he continued to exhibit his shyness around them. At a 1926 Lehigh alumnae dinner honoring Ward's gift of $1,000,000 to construct the Engineering building, Alvan Macauley touched upon Ward's demeanor as he had known him at the Packard Motor Car Company: "Mr. Packard is of rather a retiring nature, belongs to few clubs, and has not sought a wide circle of friends. He is widely known, but this is more because of his accomplishments than the result of any self-seeking. To the people who know him well he is extremely cordial, friendly, and tolerant of the views of others".

From an early age Ward's social contacts outside of the family provided less enjoyment and stimulation to him than his technical inquisitiveness. He enjoyed family life, but was unlike all four of his siblings when it came to exuberance and outside contacts. At approximately 5'2", a height similar to his brother Will, Ward was small in stature even in those days. But his intelligence and intuitive abilities were unsurpassed.

After graduation Ward had interviews with at least two companies. In August 1884 he accepted employment with the Sawyer-Man Company of New York City.

Closely identified with the Consolidated Electric Company, Sawyer-Man was a leading supplier of electrical equipment and light bulbs in those pioneering years of the Electrical Age. The company had been formed in 1879 by William Sawyer and Albon Man and by 1884 operated a very large factory in New York.

Two other entrepreneurs, Elihu Thomson and Edwin Houston, were also quick to enter the new Electrical Age. Their company, Thomson-Houston, was headquartered in Lynn, Massachusetts. In 1886 their success enabled them to purchase Sawyer-Man. The New York plant and personnel became part of Thomson-Houston. By 1890, as Ward left and returned to Warren, Thomson-Houston had become one part of the triumvirate that dominated the American electrical lighting industry. The others were Edison and Westinghouse.

When Ward reported for work on August 6, 1884 at the Sawyer-Man plant, he was assigned to work in the dynamo room (probably the factory's power plant) at $6 per week..... slightly more than ten cents an hour. Within a month he was in charge of the room. By the end of the year Ward was spending much time on the road helping with the application and installation of new electrical power plants or individual components. He was also involved with trouble-shooting those Sawyer-Man systems and components in various cities that were not performing well. His salary was now fifteen cents an hour.

A year later, in November 1885, Ward was promoted to Foreman of the Mechanical Department at a salary of $20 per week. Just before the acquisition of Sawyer-Man by Thomson-Houston, he was put in charge of the whole factory – a position he apparently held until returning to Warren.

During his years in New York Ward changed his address many times. At least six different rooms were rented in that time period with one rental including both room and board. His father would at times visit Ward in New York. Several diary entries mention meals taken with Warren at upper end restaurants in the city. One favorite was the Astor Hotel on Longacre Square-now known as Times Square. The Astor was demolished many years ago, but the building directly across Broadway that later housed an early Packard Motor Car Company factory agency still stands.

Ward's analytic mind and engineering talent continued to mature while at Sawyer-Man/Thomson-Houston. His first U.S. Patent, No. 383484-the manufacture of filaments for electric lamps-was granted on May 29, 1888. Many more would follow related to both the electrical and automotive industries.

Ward noted at the end of his 1889 diary that his total income for 1889 was $4419.80. Although unknown how much of this came from his Thomson-Houston position, it was a substantial amount for the time with a value of over $100,000 in today's debased currency. He had just passed his 26th birthday.

Both Will and Ward thought that the time was right for them to enter the electrical industry on their own. Ward resigned from Thomson-Houston and returned to Warren. Will had already put the finishing touches on a business plan for their new venture.

As Ward moved back into his parents' mansion facing the Courthouse Square on High Street, the brothers immediately put into play their plan to raise capital locally for a new electrical component manufacturing company in Warren. It would produce dynamos (generators), lamps, and other electrical equipment. The Packard Electric Company was incorporated June 5, 1890. Unfortunately, the stock sale did not meet expectations. Packard Electric could not afford to proceed beyond land acquisition and the erection of two buildings. The first building was a two story wood structure 40' x 80' and the second a single story brick structure 16' x 30'. The company's property was located on the north side of North Avenue (now Dana Street) just east of Park Avenue. Ward was president of the new company and Will was secretary/treasurer.

Even before Packard Electric's incorporation it was evident that more capital would be required to fund equipment, materials and personnel. Ward again returned to his old contacts in New York City and was successful in raising adequate additional capital to properly fund the business in Warren. However, the new investors stipulated that this new money should be separate from the initial Packard Electric capitalization. The New York and Ohio Company was thus established and incorporated on January 27, 1891. John W. Peale of New York was initially named president, Ward was general superintendent, and Will was again secretary/treasurer.

The two companies were closely allied from the first, and only a decade after their formation did they begin to significantly specialize in diverse product lines. From the beginning, Packard Electric supplied the facilities for the business and the New York & Ohio Company would provide equipment, materials, and personnel. Will would be the chief promoter, representing the New York & Ohio Company. Ward would oversee operations and technology. Ten people were initially employed. Younger sister Alaska began working in the plant during September 1891.

The electrical business kept Ward very busy. No small effort was spent attempting to suppress or circumvent the aggressive patent lawsuits initiated by the Edison interests against other producers. Judgments for these lawsuits several times stopped production of incandescent lamps at Warren in the early years, forcing Ward to abruptly change suppliers, processes and even designs. Incandescent lamp durability was also an issue in those pioneering days and Ward provided several innovations that improved the life and quality of their product.

But the electrical business did prosper and soon it was necessary to expand the company's facilities. In September 1894, as one of the first expansions, the Specialty Woodworking Company, just east of the Packard Electric property on North Avenue, was acquired by the Packard brothers for $1,300. The name was changed to the Packard Enameling Company. By November 1895 the enameling company property was sold to the Packard Electric Company for $6,000. This provided additional land and a building needed for expansion. The enameling company had operated to provide enamel paint coating for buckets, wood hardware and other miscellaneous products.

The electrical business was not Ward's only interest at that time. In February 1892 he purchased a 25' launch with a 9 horsepower internal combustion (naptha) engine for $1094.50. The new boat was housed on Lake Chautauqua at the Packard Lakewood cottages. Two years later he had completely disassembled the engine, and certainly took the opportunity to thoroughly understand its design and operation.

Also in 1892 Ward commissioned an architect to design a new three-story and basement building on the Courthouse Square Park Avenue site of the old Warren Packard home. Two of the Packard daughters had been born there before the family's 1874 move into the High Street mansion. The new building was called the Packard Block and was completed in 1894. Ward later lived in an apartment there for about two years, after the High Street mansion was closed down in 1902. The 1904 Warren City Directory lists the address as 23 ½ North Park. Ward's 1894 diary provided the final cost reconciliation of the Packard Block at $21,521.80.

Ward's inquisitive mind led him to purchase an Eastman Kodak camera and fittings in 1894 for the princely sum of $122.65. One year later he acquired a Columbia bicycle for $108.

Significantly, 1894 also provided the first mention in Ward's diary of his future wife, Elizabeth Gillmer. "Bess" was the daughter of Judge Thomas Gillmer. The highly respected Gillmer family lived near the Packards on High Street. Both families most certainly traveled in the same social circles. Elizabeth became a graduate of both Rockford and Vassar Colleges and was involved in many women's causes and intellectual activities in Warren. She probably saw Ward frequently at the Public Library where she volunteered much of her time. Ward's diary for August 31 noted, "Mother, Olive, Bess Gillmer and Finch returned to Warren on 3." Olive was twelve years old at the time and Elizabeth was twenty three. Finch was the current Packard family dog. "3" was the westbound Erie Railroad train that originated in New York and terminated in Chicago with scheduled stops in Lakewood, New York, and Warren.

Ironically, Ward and Elizabeth were married exactly ten years to the day after this diary entry.

Again in 1895 another direction that would forever change the lives of the Packard brothers would begin to unfold. Will had returned from his second European visit. This time he returned with a small gasoline-powered tricycle from France-a DeDion-Bouton.

The new French machine was crude and unreliable but this only translated as an opportunity for Ward to better understand the design and function of internal combustion engines. After dabbling with it for a period of time, it ended up as a toy for his nephew Warren II. With his interest piqued, Ward traveled to Pennsylvania in January 1896 to view a "horseless carriage"' constructed by a Dr. Booth. In May Ward's diary read, "Engaged Cowles to work on motor wagon". However, an economic downturn forced a temporary halt to that project.

In July of 1898 Ward visited Alexander Winton of Cleveland, one of the foremost pioneers in the production of horseless carriages. On August 6 Ward ordered a new Winton, number 13 of 22 produced by the Winton Motor Carriage Company that year. Returning to Cleveland a week later, he attempted to drive his new machine back to Warren. He arrived behind a team of horses at 11:00 p.m. The Winton had failed to negotiate the 65-mile trip, coming to a complete halt just three miles from Warren.

This event had several major influences on the Packard brothers' future.

The pioneering automotive story of the Packard brothers is well recorded and the subject of several other publications. Perhaps the most accurate and interesting summary of the automotive years in Warren is contained in Terry Martin's book, Packard - The Warren Years, first published in 2009.This early development story of the Packard automobile will not be included herein except for some very general timelines.

The first Packard successfully ran on the streets of Warren on November 6, 1899. A partnership agreement had been signed and formalized on July 3 between Ward, Will, and George L. Weiss of Cleveland to build a horseless carriage. Upon the success of the first carriage, plans were immediately agreed upon to build 6 or 8 more machines. Thus began the Packard automobile.

By September 1900 it was obvious that there would be a significant demand for this pioneering auto. At that time, the Ohio Automobile Company was therefore created as a corporation of West Virginia, dissolving the Packard and Weiss partnership. Significantly, necessary real estate was acquired by the new company from the Packard Electric Company for $13,000 while the machinery, tools and materials were acquired from the New York & Ohio Company for $15,600. An unknown number of personnel were also transferred from New York & Ohio to the Ohio Automobile Company. The automobile venture was now on its own.

A measure of Ward's business acumen would become evident a year later. On October 5, 1901 he penned an assignment agreement with the Ohio Automobile Company, selling to the corporation all rights to five auto related patents that had previously been granted in Ward's name (667792, 667908 thru -911). The selling price was an astronomical $30,000-about $800,000 in today's debased currency. Ward took payment as 300 shares of Ohio Auto Company stock. His portion of that sale was the foundation for a major part of the Packard family fortune in the years to come.

By 1902 more change in the automotive business was taking place. Henry B. Joy and his fellow Detroit investors had acquired a majority interest in the Ohio Automobile Company. The first change was to reincorporate the company as the Packard Motor Car Company. The auto business was flourishing and these investors had been required to several times add new capital to expand the business. The decision was made to move the business from Warren to Detroit. A new plant was built on the Grand Boulevard in Detroit. The Packard Motor Car Company officially closed the doors in Warren on October 10, 1903.

Ward was in Detroit during this transition but abruptly returned on October 9th due to the sudden death of his mother.

Will had resigned as a Director in the company at the time of the move while Ward remained as director and president, although the latter was more or less an honorary position. Henry Joy was now the General Manager and he was definitely in charge. In 1908 Ward was named Chairman of the Board, a position that was eliminated by the Packard Board of Directors in 1912. Ward finally resigned as a director in May 1915. He had, for all practical purposes, not been active in the company since December 1903.

The success and prestige ultimately bestowed on the Packard Motor Car Company during the first several decades of its existence can be attributed to the leadership and philosophies of business imparted by its first three presidents: James Ward Packard, Henry Bourne Joy and James Alvan Macauley.

In 1904, soon after the automobile operations left Warren, changes took place as well at the New York & Ohio Company. Ward had been General Manager. Will's main business effort had been the marketing and sale of their products. Now the company was integrated into the National Electric Lamp Association (NELA) and focused on manufacturing incandescent light bulbs. The brothers would remain involved, but change was in the wind-General Electric purchased the company in 1911. The operation became the Ohio Lamp Works of General Electric. The plant ceased operations in December 2013.

The Packard Electric Company became specialized in electrical componentry for the rapidly growing automotive industry. In 1906 Newton Wolcott was named General Manager of the company-Ward retained the title of president until 1916 when he resigned and Wolcott replaced him. In 1932 Packard Electric became a division of General Motors Corporation.

Ward had retained substantial holdings in both Packard Electric and the New York & Ohio companies, just as he had in the Packard automotive business. The standard of living ultimately enjoyed by tens of thousands of families who worked in these Packard-created businesses is a testament to the creativity and hard work of the brothers. There is no better example of the benefits of free market capitalism than the success of the Packard businesses in the century of their existence.

Other events were also occupying Ward's attention during these years of electrical and automotive pioneering. In December 1900 he had purchased his second launch from the S.S. & I. Boat Company for $1900. This one featured a 6" x 6" Howard motor. Again in June 1902, Will's diary mentioned another new boat for Ward at Lakewood. Significantly, Will's diary in May 1903 also mentions the purchase for Ward of a Schumann Repeater for $25.....possibly the first pocket watch in a collection that grew to be arguably the best ever assembled in America.

By January 1902, Ward also completed construction of the Packard Apartments at 157-159 Park Avenue (now 300-318 Park Avenue North). While the rest of the Packard family moved into these luxurious apartments from the High Street mansion, Ward chose to take up residence at his Packard Block on the Courthouse Square. He would live there in his second floor apartment for almost two years.

On August 31, 1904 life again changed profoundly for Ward. On that date he married Elizabeth A. Gillmer. They were married soon after Elizabeth returned from two years of teaching in the Phoenix, Arizona public schools. The wedding was held at

James Ward Packard, Successful Businessman

James Ward & Elizabeth (Gillmer) Packard on their honeymoon at the Panama Rocks, a tourist attraction on Lake Chautauqua near Lakewood, New York. They were married in Warren on 31 August, 1904. The car is a 1904 Packard Model L.

the Gillmer home on High Street and was a complete surprise to many friends and acquaintances of the couple. After a brief honeymoon at the Packard cottage on Lake Chautauqua in Lakewood, they returned to take up residence in the Packard Block apartment. Ward was 41 years old and Elizabeth was 33. They would have an active and harmonious marriage for the next 24 years.

In 1905 the newlyweds purchased the old W.W. Abell house at 185 Park Avenue (now 366 Park Avenue North). This was just north of the Packard Apartments. The couple extensively remodeled the house and lived there continuously until 1924. Today this building houses the Buckeye Club. Ward's basement hobby room is still essentially intact.

Almost immediately Ward and Elizabeth began planning for their new summer home on Terrace Street in Lakewood. This involved much greater effort and began with the moving of several buildings from the site, including the large Twin Cottages that had been built in the 1890's by the Packard brothers on the shore of Lake Chautauqua. These were moved intact to new sites south of Terrace. By 1910 the property was ready to accept a new Packard lakeshore mansion with extensive surrounding landscaped grounds. The new mansion was constructed in 1911-12. Ward and Elizabeth were able to move in during 1912 with the necessary support staff. This became the Packard's summer home. After Ward's death in 1928 it became the primary residence of Elizabeth until her death in 1960. It is today the centerpiece of a condominium complex which has been developed on the site.

Ward and Elizabeth indulged their personal interests and avocations during the second decade of the 20th century. Ward only briefly re-entered the business world. In 1916 he purchased the Buffalo, New York auto agency from the Packard Motor Car Company of New York. For several years the dealership sold both Packard and Liberty autos, then was sold again. It was a brief affair for the absentee owner. Apparently it did not generate any continuing interest from Ward.

Again in the early 1920's Ward and Elizabeth decided to build another new home. This new home was in their hometown of Warren. In 1924 they moved into their beautiful new Georgian-design mansion on Oak Knoll. Today it is still a private residence.

Elizabeth Gillmer
Probably about the time of her wedding to James Ward Packard

Tragedy soon entered Ward's life. In January 1926 he underwent abdominal cancer surgery. For a short period of time it appeared that the malignancy had been eliminated but within a few months it reappeared. By November 1926 Ward had returned to the Cleveland Clinic for further treatment. He would never leave the hospital again. After sixteen agonizing months he passed away on March 20, 1928. He was 64 years old.

It was during these final months confined in the hospital that Ward planned most of his philanthropic gifts. Elizabeth was with him constantly. She passed the days reading to him. His last and grandest pocket watch, one whose complications he had specified for watchmaker Patek Philippe & Co.-Geneva in 1922, only arrived while he was in the hospital in 1927. The watch with all its grand complications is still known to this day as "The Packard". He was never able to truly enjoy its many fine details.

Ward was buried in Section 2, Lot 119, at Oakwood Cemetery. This was not the original Packard burial plot in Oakwood. Ward and Elizabeth had decided to buy a separate one. Lot 119 is adjacent to the Gillmer family plot of Elizabeth's parents.

Elizabeth died at Lakewood on January 19, 1960 at 88 years of age. She is buried next to Ward in Oakwood Cemetery.

Chapter 5

The Girls — Alaska, Carlotta and Olive

After the birth of Will and Ward, next in line were the three girls who would round out the family of Warren and Mary Doud Packard. They all developed their own individual strengths and traits and were extremely devoted to family. The girls shared the gift of broader out-of-family sociability with Will. All would follow their own path in life, but would come together with the family when called to collectively share their happiness or grief.

The girls exhibited their own particular and distinct personalities.

Alaska would have been characterized as "the leader of the pack". She was always out in front whether in conversation or her own personal initiatives.

Carlotta evolved as the active socialite among the girls. Always ready to help members of her family, she nevertheless moved to New York City to pursue a decadent life in a rarer social circle.

Olive remained more closely connected and became a lifelong society matron in Cleveland. She buried two husbands and quickly divorced a third. She thoroughly enjoyed extensive travel throughout her life.

Surprisingly, the five children of Warren and Mary Doud Packard did not produce a plethora of grandchildren for them to enjoy. Will and Annie were the parents of Warren II (1892-1929). Alaska and E. B. McCrum parented daughter Esther (1894-1902). Henry Packard White (1909-1974) was the only child of Olive and Carl White.

Both Warren and Mary never knew Olive's son and, due to severe physical or mental problems throughout her short life, probably saw very little of Alaska's daughter. The generation beyond the five Packard siblings was thin indeed.

Alaska

Alaska Packard at about 20 years of age.

The third child of Warren and Mary Doud Packard, Alaska was the first daughter born to them. The Packards again relied on choosing a significant given name for their baby....this time it was to honor the purchase of Alaska from the Russians.

The acquisition had been concluded in March 1867. The $7,000,000 purchase price worked out to be just about two cents an acre for this cold and remote land. President Andrew Johnson's political enemies took aim at his Secretary of State, William Seward, and delighted in calling this blatant waste of government money "Seward's Folly".

But apparently Warren Packard's political loyalties were with Johnson. The Packard daughter was born on March 1, 1868 in the Packard family home on Park Avenue, at the current location of the Packard Block. She was named Alaska and would become known as "Al" for her entire life.

Al was a leader and frequently seemed to be on the front edge of any situation, for better or for worse. While she attended the Warren Public Schools for a period of time, she was the only Packard sibling that did not continue her education in some form beyond Warren.

As a child Al was devoted to her family, particularly to her younger sister Carlotta. They traveled in more or less the same circles. Both seemed to enjoy the animals, particularly dogs, that were always a part of the Packard family.

By 1891, at age 23, Al was an employee of the New York & Ohio Company. Mid 1893 newspaper accounts listed her as being in charge of the factory which at that time had over 100 employees. Other accounts stated that she was a foreman which was quite an unusual situation for a woman of the Victorian era. All that would change abruptly in late 1893.

On November 7 Al married Ephraim Banks (E.B.) McCrum, Jr. at the Warren Packard mansion on High Street. E.B. had been a groomsman for Will's 1891 wedding to Annie Storer and Al was a bridesmaid for Annie. At that time he was listed as cashier for the Paige Tube Company, a business located on North Avenue adjacent to the Pennsylvania Railroad line. Paige Tube produced wrought iron pipe and well casings at that location throughout most of the 1890's. By 1893 he was listed as secretary of Paige. After their honeymoon, the McCrums set up housekeeping in June 1894 on Washington Avenue in Warren. They later moved to Akron.

Their only child, Esther, was born on November 20, 1894. Tragically, Esther suffered from severe handicaps and was committed to the Institution for Feeble-Minded Youth in Columbus, Ohio before her sixth birthday. She died there of pneumonia on April 20, 1902. She was buried in the Paltzgroff family plot of Paltzgroff Cemetery, Lordstown. Her grandmother, Mary Elizabeth Doud Packard, as well as Al many years later, would follow Esther to that resting place.

Matters were not sublime in the McCrum household. Al filed for divorce from E.B., which was granted September 10, 1900. This was a very radical step to be taken in the early 20th century. She moved back into the Packard mansion on High Street and again began working at the New York and Ohio Company. E.B. died of tuberculosis in August 1908 and is buried in Oak Hill Cemetery, Youngstown.

On July 12, 1905 Al remarried, this time to James B. Davidson, at the Packard cottage in Lakewood, New York. Although Mr. Davidson was originally from Warren, they started life together in Pittsburgh. They later moved to a farm near Accotink, Virginia, where they bred horses and dogs. Mr. Davidson died May 3, 1929. He is buried in the Davidson family plot in Oakwood Cemetery, Warren.

After the Davidsons moved to Accotink (near Washington, D.C.), Al exhibited her leading edge persona one more time… at age 54 she is recognized as being the first female Special Agent to have served in the Federal Bureau of Investigation (FBI), from October 1922 until June 1924. When J. Edgar Hoover became director of the FBI in May 1924, he was not supportive of female special agents and asked for Al's resignation. Not until 1972 would women again be accepted for this position. Her remaining years were spent at the Accotink farm where she continued to raise dogs.

Al succumbed to complications from gallstone surgery on July 16, 1934 at age 65. She was buried alongside her mother and daughter at the Paltzgroff Cemetery in Lordstown. She had experienced life to the fullest.

Alaska Packard Davidson
during her FBI days – 1922 to 1924

Carlotta

The next child of Warren and Mary Doud Packard was another daughter, this one named Carlotta. There appears to be no significance to this name chosen for the fourth sibling. She was the second and last Packard born at the Packard home on Park Avenue overlooking Warren's Courthouse Square. The date was April 6, 1869.

Carlotta attended the Warren Public Schools then rounded out her education at a finishing school in Bethlehem, Pennsylvania. This reflected her upper middle class status – a typical path followed by young ladies from prosperous families in the late 19th century.

Carlotta Packard with
young nephew Warren II & Towser ca. 1895

Carlotta Packard in New York City, 1931, with her dog Chico

After returning from school in the East, Carlotta again settled into the family mansion on High Street. For the next fifteen years she would focus on family. For several periods of time was the main caregiver for her father, her mother and – briefly – for young nephew Warren II.

In addition to her close bond with sister Alaska, Carlotta also shared love and companionship with her much younger sister during Olive's teenage years in the 1890's. The decade was spent with frequent travel to visit relatives as far away as New England and New York, and to the comfort of summers spent at the family property in Lakewood.

Carlotta was an enthusiastic lover of dogs. For her entire life she was involved with the family's pets. In 1895 she acquired Towser in Canada. This dark medium sized dog of questionable origin was her devoted companion for over a decade until Carlotta moved to New York City around 1907. In addition to being immortalized in photographs with early Packard autos, Towser also sat for a formal portrait with his mistress and her young nephew Warren II. He was well known around Warren. The local newspaper carried a detailed obituary upon his death in July 1908. His demise was attributed in large measure to a broken heart due to Carlotta's departure from Warren.

Care for family members and an active social life filled Carlotta's days in the late Victorian era. She and Ward seemed to share the keeping of the family dogs between them. Towser is known to have traveled frequently on the train between Warren and Lakewood, especially during the summer seasons.

Will had married Annie in 1891, and Carlotta's close bond with her older sister was loosened a few years later by Al's marriage to E.B. McCrum and Esther's arrival in the McCrum household. While still very close as a family, sibling marriages had changed the equation. Carlotta spent more time with her father, mother and much younger sibling Olive–still not deciding a course for her life. In September 1897 she went to work at the New York & Ohio Company factory. This was not the kind of life she desired and her employment there was not long.

The remaining Packard family moved out of the cavernous High Street mansion and into the luxurious new Packard Apartments on Park Avenue in April 1902. This would remain Carlotta's home for the next five years or so.

Before her 40th birthday, Carlotta decided to move into the social circles of New York City. By the early 1930's she had moved into the new apartment building at 22 Riverside Drive between West 74th and 75th Streets on Manhattan's upper west side. 22 Riverside was and still is an imposing 19-story luxury apartment building with a front view of the Hudson River, and Central Park as a back yard a few blocks away. Carlotta's socialite neighbors included Charles Schwab, one of the founders of Bethlehem Steel and several times savior of the Stutz Motor Car Company in Indianapolis.

Another attraction of the Riverside Drive neighborhood was the dog park located two blocks from her apartment. This was ideal for walking Chico, her Belgian Griffon dog. She lived the idyllic life of a wealthy socialite in New York for over 30 years.

Carlotta died of heart failure in New York on December 3, 1940. She was 71 years old and was the ninth Packard to be buried in the Oakwood Cemetery family plot. Unlike all her siblings, she never married.

Cornelia Olive

Olive "Little Packard," ca. 1884

The fifth and last child of the Packards was another daughter, named Cornelia Olive. She was born on June 29, 1882, over thirteen years since last sister Carlotta's birth. Brother Will, her oldest sibling, was 20; father, Warren was 54, and mother Mary Doud was 43 years old. It must have come as a real surprise to the whole family to welcome another addition into the Packard household at that late date.

Olive was the only Packard born in the mansion on High Street. In her youth she was affectionately tagged "Little Packard" by her siblings. The moniker that stayed with her throughout her life was "Polly". She readily identified herself that way in communications within the family.

Olive enjoyed the attention and care of her family. She had a loving and privileged childhood. However, her father Warren died when she was only fifteen years old in 1897.

Two years later she left Warren to attend the Dana Hall School in Wellesley, Massachusetts. Dana Hall is a high end women's private finishing school which provided Olive with a social polish much like that obtained by older sister Carlotta.

She graduated in June 1902 and returned to Warren after making a brief visit to England–her first of many trips to Europe. It was said that Olive visited England 17 times during her lifetime. She circumnavigated the globe three times. Her trips to England in later years quite likely included visits with her brother Will's granddaughter, Rosalie.

Rosalie had married an Englishman. She had happily resettled to the upper-end Kensington district of metropolitan London, where she spent the rest of her life. When she died her remains were returned to Warren and are now buried in the Packard family plot in Oakwood Cemetery. Rosalie and her brother Warren Packard III are the tenth and eleventh burials in the family plot originally purchased by their great-grandfather Warren Packard in 1855.

After returning from school and this first European trek, Olive's home was different from the one she had left in 1899. Early in 1902 the family had closed the cavernous mansion on High Street. They now lived in one unit of the Packard Apartments on Park Avenue. Olive called this home along with her mother and Carlotta. At this time, Brother Will and his son Warren II occupied a separate apartment there with housekeeper Kitty Bruder. Another unit was occupied by Uncle Benjamin Franklin Packard and his wife Mary.

More significant changes would come rapidly in Olive's life. In October 1903 her mother died. Less than a year later, in August 1904, brother Ward was wed to Elizabeth Gillmer in Elizabeth's family home. In July 1905 Al's second marriage, to James Davidson, was solemnized at the Packard cottage in Lakewood.

Then came Olive's own wedding on June 5, 1906 to Carl Foster White of Cleveland. The wedding took place at brother Will's brand new home, River Court, on Mahoning Avenue. Carl White was a prominent architect in Cleveland. He was a cousin to the family members with both

Carl Foster White, Olive's first husband

(Photos courtesy of Dorothy Gilliam.)

Olive Packard White at the time of her wedding

the White Sewing Machine Company and the White (Automobile) Company in Cleveland. The couple would immediately establish their residence on East 89th Street in Cleveland, right around the corner from Euclid Avenue which was referred to as Millionaire's Row. Olive's life as a prominent socialite matron began with this marriage. She was not yet 24 years old. The Warren newspaper description of the wedding disclosed the participants and guests, but there was no mention of Kitty Bruder. Will and Kitty would also be married, at Ward's Lakewood cottage, soon after Olive's wedding in 1906.

With her wedding to Carl White, Olive's residency in Cleveland would be permanent for the remaining 60 years of her life, with short winter interludes in Florida.

Olive's first child, Henry Packard White was born on April 29, 1909. For most of his adult life Henry owned and operated a very successful physical testing laboratory. Olive gave birth to a second child on April 20, 1913 but the baby was stillborn or died within several hours. Their father Carl died of pneumonia two days before Henry's sixth birthday in 1915 and is buried in the White family plot in Lake View Cemetery, Cleveland. Olive would be interred with him in 1966. Their son would join them both in 1974.

Olive's second marriage on September 23, 1916 was to another prominent Cleveland businessman, oil executive and commodities broker Guy Stewart Gardner. Their marriage lasted until his death on March 22, 1939 in Sarasota, Florida. He was 65 years old. Guy was buried in Woodlawn Cemetery, Cleveland.

Olive married in Cleveland for a third time to Percy Warner Tinan, on November 23, 1940. Mr. Tinan had been married twice before and had divorced his second wife in Mexico only 16 days before his marriage to Olive. Apparently this third union wasn't made in heaven either. Olive soon dissolved it. She started using the Gardner name again for the rest of her life.

The 50th anniversary of the first Packard automobile was commemorated in Warren in November 1949. Olive made a visit to her old hometown to participate in the dedication of a tablet to mark the event. Visits to Warren were now few and far between. At the end, Olive was the last of her generation of Packards.

Olive died on March 9, 1966 in Cleveland of injuries sustained in a house fire. She was 83 years old.

Olive married her second husband, Guy Gardner, in September 1916. He was a prominent Cleveland businessman. Guy died of a heart attack in Sarasota, Florida in March 1939.

Percy Warner Tinan, Olive Packard's 3rd husband. Born in Painesville, Ohio on 8 October 1880, he purchased the automobile business of George W. Blackmore of Painesville in 1905. Blackmore had owned a dealership representing Olds, Orient, Winton, and Packard, and had originally purchased Packard Model B No. A-30 in August 1900. He became a dealer for Packard a month later. Prior to his brief marriage to Olive in 1940, Tinan had been listed as a Publicity Agent.

Olive Packard Gardner at the dedication of tablet marking the 50th Anniversary of the Packard Automobile, Warren, Ohio, November 1949. (L to R): George Woodside; Henry Schryver, a Packard employee and machinist who worked on the first Packard car; Mrs. Katherine Summers, niece of Mrs. James Ward (Elizabeth Gillmer) Packard; Hugh Ferry. Executive Vice-President of the Packard Motor Car Co.; and Mrs. Olive Packard Gardner, sister of James Ward & William Doud Packard.

Chapter 6

Warren II — The Last Generation from Warren, Ohio

Warren and Mary Doud Packard must have felt confident that they would be surrounded by many loving grandchildren as the 1890's unfolded. Both Will and Al had married early in the decade and both had a child by 1895. Sadly, only one of these children would live to adulthood and no more children would be born to Will or Al.

The next round of four family marriages would take place between 1904 and 1906 after the death of both Warren and Mary. This round included all of the Packard siblings except Carlotta, who never married. These four marriages would produce only one offspring–Henry Packard White, Olive's son. Henry's hometown was Cleveland. He never felt any real connection to the Packard family of Warren.

Warren Packard II ca. 1902

The only Packard of the Warren, Ohio clan who lived to maturity was Will and Annie's son, Warren II. Born October 5, 1892 in the family home on Elm Street, young Warren lost his mother at age three to complications from appendicitis. With father Will frequently away from home on business, much of young Warren's youth was spent in the care of his two grandmothers and his Aunt Carlotta. Will's 1906 marriage to Kathryn Bruder gave him a new stepmother in his teenage years.

Warren II attended the Warren Public Schools. In 1907 he was enrolled in Culver Military Academy for the completion of his high school years. He then attended Cornell University. In 1914 he obtained a degree in Electrical Engineering.

Returning to Warren, he worked at Packard Electric Company until volunteering in the U.S. Navy during the Great War. He was discharged in 1919, then moved to Cleveland to organize the Packard Engineering Company, a distributor for Lovejoy Shock Absorbers – a popular accessory for automobiles in that era.

Henry Packard White ca. 1960. Son of Carl F. and Olive (Packard) White

In August 1920 he married Dorothy Braden in Akron, Ohio. By 1926 they had two children, Rosalie (1924-1998) and Warren III (1926-2011).

In early 1923 Warren became employed by the Packard Motor Car Company in Detroit at a beginning salary of $125 a month. By 1926 he was Advertising and Sales Promotion Manager for Packard's Detroit Sales and Service Branch. He was also a recently licensed pilot.

On August 26, 1929 Warren was participating in a Packard Salesman's Convention in Detroit. Much to the delight of many of the conventioneers, during the day he landed a single engine amphibious plane on the Detroit River. Taking off from the river later again that day, he lost control of the plane north of Detroit and crashed into marshes near the river. He was killed in the mishap. He was the seventh Packard to be buried in the family plot at Oakwood Cemetery, Warren.

He was also the last member of his Packard line to be born and raised in Warren. Warren II's descendants live on through the children of his son, Warren Packard III.

Warren II & Dorothy (Braden) Packard (at left in photo). Photographed in 1929 standing in front of the prototype Packard Monoblock Twelve Custom Victoria.

The last picture – a treasured memory of the many Master Salesmen who knew Warren Packard, Killed on the Convention's first day a few hours after this was snapped, which shows Warren characteristically doing something for Packard as part of the 1929 Convention program.

Packard Inner Circle
December 21, 1929

Chapter 7

The Packard Homes in Warren

When Warren Packard first arrived in Warren in 1846 he boarded with Milton Graham and his family. Census records from 1850 indicate that he was by then boarding with the family of Edward E. Hoyt.

It is a fair assumption that Warren began living in a rental home on the northwest corner of Elm and East Market Streets in Warren at about the time of his first marriage to Sylvia Camp, in 1852. The residence was documented on an 1856 Trumbull County / Warren plat map which illustrates all occupied buildings of that time. The W. Packard residence was listed as #12 on Market Street.

Tragically, Sylvia and the two boys born of this first marriage had all died within six short years. Warren married again, this time to Mary Elizabeth Doud, in 1860. He still lived in the Market Street house and it is known that their first two children – Will and Ward – were both born here.

No known photograph or image of this house has apparently yet been discovered. The Packard family were tenants for at least three years.

The next home was probably the first one owned by Warren and Mary Packard. This was located on Courthouse Square in Warren and, again, no photo or view of this home is known. Both Alaska and Carlotta were born here in the late 1860's. An insurance record from the early 1870's outlines theirs as a fairly significant property on the square. This site was redeveloped in the 1890's by Ward and is known as the Packard Block.

From the time the Packard family moved into the large new mansion at #2 High Street, photo records of that and all subsequent Packard homes in Warren are available and are included herein.

Also included herein are photos of the last homes of Alaska (Fairfax County, Virginia), Carlotta (New York City) and Olive (Cleveland).

The first investment property developed by Ward Packard was the Packard Block located on the east side of Park Avenue on Courthouse Square, in the center of Warren. He engaged prominent New Castle architect S.W. Faulk to design the new site.

The Warren Packard Home

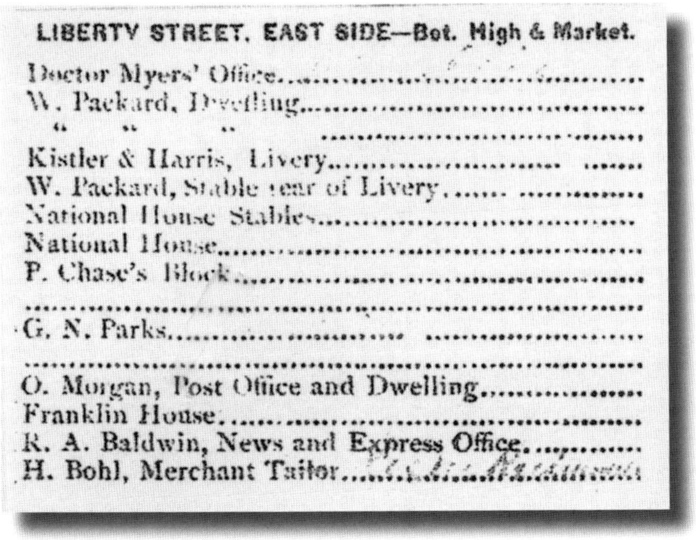
LIBERTY STREET, EAST SIDE—Bet. High & Market.

Doctor Myers' Office....................................
W. Packard, Dwelling....................................
" " "....................................
Kistler & Harris, Livery....................................
W. Packard, Stable rear of Livery....................................
National House Stables....................................
National House....................................
P. Chase's Block....................................
....
G. N. Parks....................................
....
O. Morgan, Post Office and Dwelling....................................
Franklin House....................................
R. A. Baldwin, News and Express Office....................................
H. Bohl, Merchant Tailor....................................

On Liberty Street (now Park Avenue), Courthouse Square
– And later –
Site of the Packard Block, 23-25 Park Avenue (now 144 N. Park Ave.)

No images of Warren Packard's home on Liberty Street are known. This is the house where Alaska (b. 1868) and Carlotta (b. 1869) were born. This same location would be deeded to son Ward in the early 1890s. The Packard family had moved into their High Street mansion in 1876.

Description of the properties on east side of Liberty Street facing the Courthouse Square – early 1870s. Listing is from High Street (north end) to Market Street (south end).

The Packard Block

In 1898

Today

Construction of this three story building began in April 1894 and was fully finished slightly less than a year later. Total cost was $21,500.

During 1895 the building was taken over for use as a temporary home for the Trumbull County Common Pleas Court due to a fire which had destroyed the courthouse across the street. A new courthouse was constructed on the same site and the court's offices were removed from the Packard Block by 1897.

Ward lived in an apartment on the second floor of the Packard Block after the High Street mansion was vacated in 1902. He remained here until early 1905, having purchased the old Abell house further north on Park Avenue. This was around the time of his marriage to Elizabeth Gillmer in August 1904.

The Packard Block today still houses businesses vital to the community. It remained part of the Packard estate until Elizabeth's death in 1960.

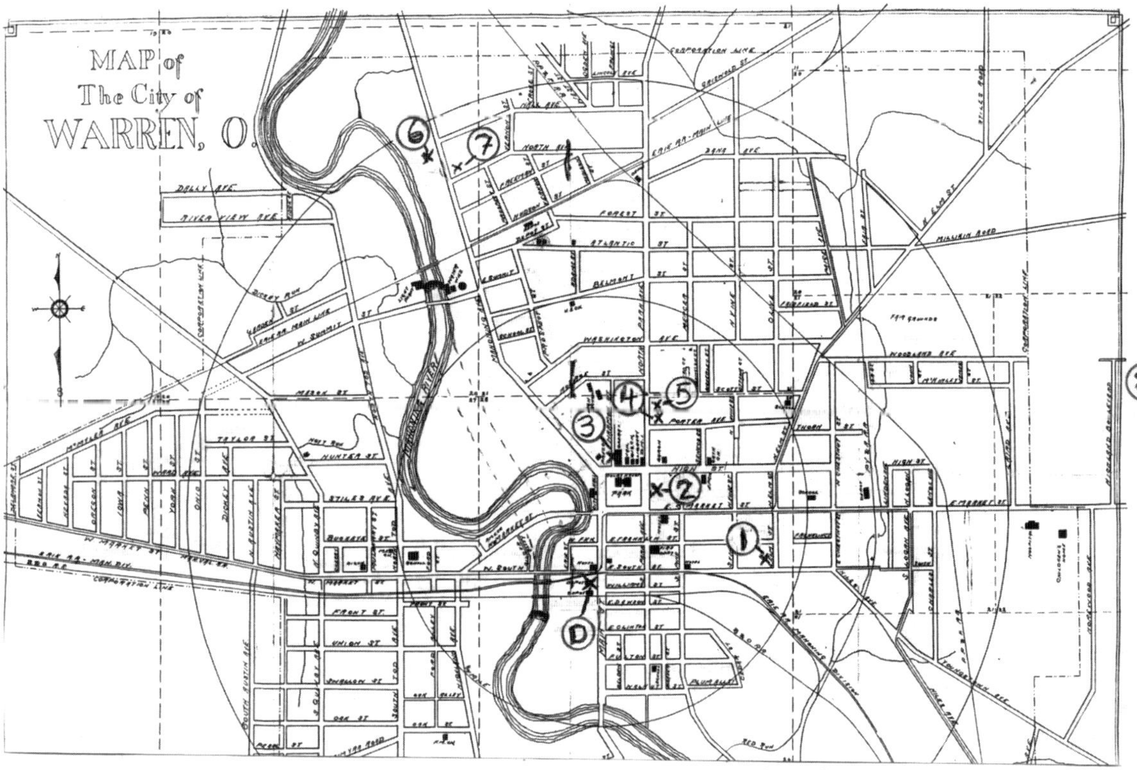

1- Warren Packard's rental home on northeast corner of E. Market St. and N. Elm St.
William Doud (b. 1861) and James Ward (b. 1863) born in this home.
Will & Annie (Storer) Packard lived in this area at 7 N. Elm St. (ca. 1891-95)

2- Warren Packard home on east side of Park Avenue, Courthouse Square
Alaska (b. 1868) and Carlotta (b. 1869) born in this home.
Ward lived in an apartment on the 2nd floor of the Packard Block. 23 1/2 N. Park Ave., 1902-05.

3- Warren Packard mansion, #2 High Street, across from Courthouse Square
Occupied by the Packard family 1876-1902.
Olive (b. 1882) born in this house.
All of the Packards (3 generations) lived at one time or another in this house.

4- Packard Apartments, Park Ave - on northeast corner of Park & Porter Ave.
Occupied by Mary Doud Packard and all of her children except Ward at various times 1902 and beyond.

5 - James Ward & Elizabeth (Gillmer) Packard residence,
185 Park Ave, SE corner of Park Ave. & Scott Street, 1905-24.

6 - William Doud & Kathryn (Bruder) Packard residence, "River Court," Mahoning Avenue, 1906-20

7 - William Doud & Kathryn (Bruder) Packard residence, "Packard Place,"
NE corner of North Street & Mahoning Avenue, 1920-40.

8 - James Ward & Elizabeth (Gillmer) Packard residence.
100 Oak Knoll Drive, NW corner of Oak Knoll & Montclair Street, 1924-28.

D- Atlantic & Great Western/Erie Railroad passenger and freight depot, SW corner of South Street & Main Street

Warren & Mary Elizabeth (Doud) Packard Home

Northeast Corner of Mahoning Avenue & High Street
2 High Street (site now occupied by YMCA addition)

Warren Packard purchased a large lot with existing structures next to the First Presbyterian Church on High Street in 1870. Construction was started in 1874 on an imposing new mansion. During 1876 the Packard family moved in.

The mansion was designed in the French Mansard style and served as the family home until 1902. The home was then rented to Harriet Taylor Upton as the national headquarters of the Womens' Suffrage Movement. On 1 January 1906 it became the home of Hall's Music Store, then a restaurant, and – finally – home to the Warren Elks Lodge No. 295 until being razed in 1963.

The site was then occupied by an extension of the adjoining YMCA building. The only remaining vestige of the Packard days is a short strip of driveway between the sidewalk and the new building.

The Packard Apartments

Northeast Corner of Park Avenue & Porter Avenue
157-159 Park Avenue (now 300-318 N. Park Avenue)

Conceived by Ward Packard as a future home for his mother and younger sisters, as well as an ongoing investment, the Packard Apartments were available for occupancy by early 1902. Ward had purchased the property in February 1901 - (2) corner lots for which he had paid $50 per front foot.

Architect S.W. Faulk, who had designed the Packard Block in 1893, was commissioned in April 1901 to create high-end apartments, and he designed fourteen suites ranging from (3) to (10) spacious rooms each. A restaurant was originally planned to be placed in the basement. Construction commenced immediately, and the units were ready for occupancy in early 1902.

Will, young Warren II and housekeeper Kitty Bruder were the first of the Packards to move in, by mid-January 1902. The widow Mary Doud Packard, along with Carlotta and Olive, moved to their new apartment from the High Street mansion in April. All of the surviving Packard family, except Ward, would subsequently live at the Packard Apartments at one time or another.

Although still standing, the Packard Apartments are currently abandoned and in deplorable condition.

James Ward & Elizabeth (Gillmer) Packard Home

Southeast Corner of Park Avenue & Scott Street
185 Park Avenue (now 366 N. Park Avenue)

The Park Avenue home as it would have appeared when the Packards moved in.

Ward Packard's hobby room in the basement, from a 1911 photograph. In addition to displaying his collected mechanical items, he had a frieze painted around the room depicting idealized ca. 1907 Packards.

At about the time of their marriage Ward & Bess purchased and completely renovated the 65-year-old W.W. Abell house, moving in during 1905. They lived here until constructing their Oak Knoll home in 1924. Beginning in 1912, they maintained dual residences in both Warren and Lakewood, New York.

This Park Avenue property is now the home of Warren's Buckeye Club.

William Doud & Kathryn (Bruder) Packard Home
"River Court"

North Mahoning Avenue (now 1375 Mahoning Avenue NW)

Will's new home, River Court, between Mahoning Avenue and the Mahoning River.

The architect for River Court was David L. Stine from Toledo.

With a massive pipe organ and pleasing views of the Mahoning River on 1 ½ acre lot, this remained the comfortable Warren home of Will and Kitty until he built "Packard Place" in 1920. Will also had built "Packard Manor" on Lake Chautauqua, New York in 1916 as a second home.

River Court was demolished in 1967 and replaced by an apartment complex. The only surviving external fragment of this beautiful old home is the left side entrance pillar adjacent to the driveway off Mahoning Avenue.

Interior view at River Court – a sun room facing the Mahoning River.

William Doud & Kathryn (Bruder) Packard Home
"Packard Place"

Northeast Corner of North Avenue & Mahoning Ave. (now 1320 Mahoning Ave.)

Constructed in 1920, "Packard Place" was Will's replacement for "River Court," which was located across Mahoning Avenue.

The design of Packard Place resembled Will's Lake Chautauqua home "Packard Manor" built in 1916, but on a smaller scale. Several small homes and outbuildings were also constructed at this site facing both North Avenue and at the back of the property. Kitty's family lived there for a period of time.

Will died at Packard Place in November 1923. Kitty chose to remain in Warren, and divested the Lake Chautauqua property. She also died at Packard Place, in February 1940.

The home is now a nursing facility and retains much of its original appearance.

James Ward & Elizabeth (Gillmer) Packard Home

Northwest Corner of Oak Knoll & Montclair Street
100 Oak Knoll Drive (Now 319 Oak Knoll Avenue NE)

Ward and Elizabeth purchased a large lot on Oak Knoll Drive, bounded on the south by Montclair Street and on the east by Roselawn Avenue, building a large Georgian-style mansion on the property in 1924. Behind the house were extensive gardens laid out by Elizabeth. It is probable that the local architectural firm O'Brian & Keich designed the Oak Knoll home.

Ward was able to enjoy his new home for only (2) years. In 1926 he entered the Cleveland Clinic, where he required hospitalization until his death in March, 1928. Elizabeth soon elected to establish her permanent residence at their home in Lakewood, and she turned the Oak Knoll property over to her niece Katherine Summers.

The home remains a private residence to this day.

Last Homes of the Packard Girls — Alaska, Carlotta & Olive

Alaska Packard Davidson's Farm

Fairfax County, Virginia

Alaska purchased this farm from the estate of Ebenezer Mason in March, 1911. At a price of $4,000, the farm included 103 acres situated directly south of the Richmond-Washington Highway (U.S. 1), plus this house called Independence Lodge. It is located approximately (3) miles west of George Washington's Mt. Vernon home.

Upon Alaska's death in 1934 the property was willed jointly to her (2) sisters Carlotta and Olive, with the wish that it be transferred to Olive's son Henry Packard White. That wish was granted, and Mr. White in turn sold the property in March 1939. The house was razed sometime after 1947.

This image of Independence Lodge appeared on Christmas cards sent by Al in December 1932. It is reproduced here through the courtesy of the Alexandria Monthly Meeting of the Religious Society of Friends.

Carlotta Packard's Apartment

22 Riverside Drive, New York City

Carlotta lived in this luxury high rise until her death in 1940. 22 Riverside Drive faces the Hudson River, and is still considered a top New York City address. Her New York addresses prior to the 1930s had included West 130th Street, West End Avenue and West 75th Street.

Olive Packard Gardner's Home

Cleveland Heights, Ohio

Still in use as a private residence.

Chapter 8

The Warren-Lakewood Connection

Warren Packard discovered the pleasant surroundings of Lake Chautauqua in New York State early in the 1870's. Thanks to the railroad connecting Warren and Lakewood/Jamestown, he was able to travel the 125 miles between them with relative ease.

The established Atlantic & Great Western rail line linked Warren and Lakewood with less than five hours of travel time. Given the roads of the day, travelers would have expected such a distance to require several days on horseback.

Packard family presence in Lakewood spanned more than 85 years, beginning with Warren's purchase of property and an interest in the Lakeview Hotel there in 1874. Through the years the A & GW would become part of the Erie System. The railroad would remain the only comfortable conduit of travel by the family until the development of automobiles and accompanying good roads.

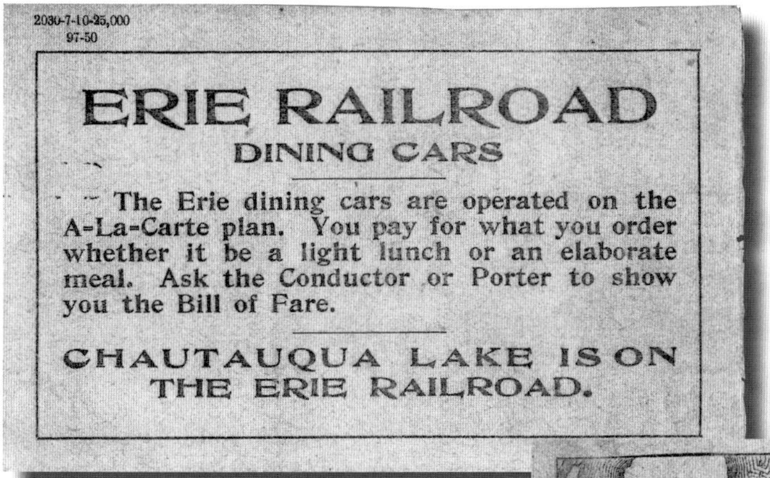

2030-7-10-25,000
97-50

ERIE RAILROAD

DINING CARS

The Erie dining cars are operated on the A-La-Carte plan. You pay for what you order whether it be a light lunch or an elaborate meal. Ask the Conductor or Porter to show you the Bill of Fare.

CHAUTAUQUA LAKE IS ON THE ERIE RAILROAD.

The Erie Railroad System – New York & Chicago Line

1907 map of Erie Line connecting Chicago and New York. Leavittsburg, Warren, Lakewood and Jamestown are all identified as stops on this main line.

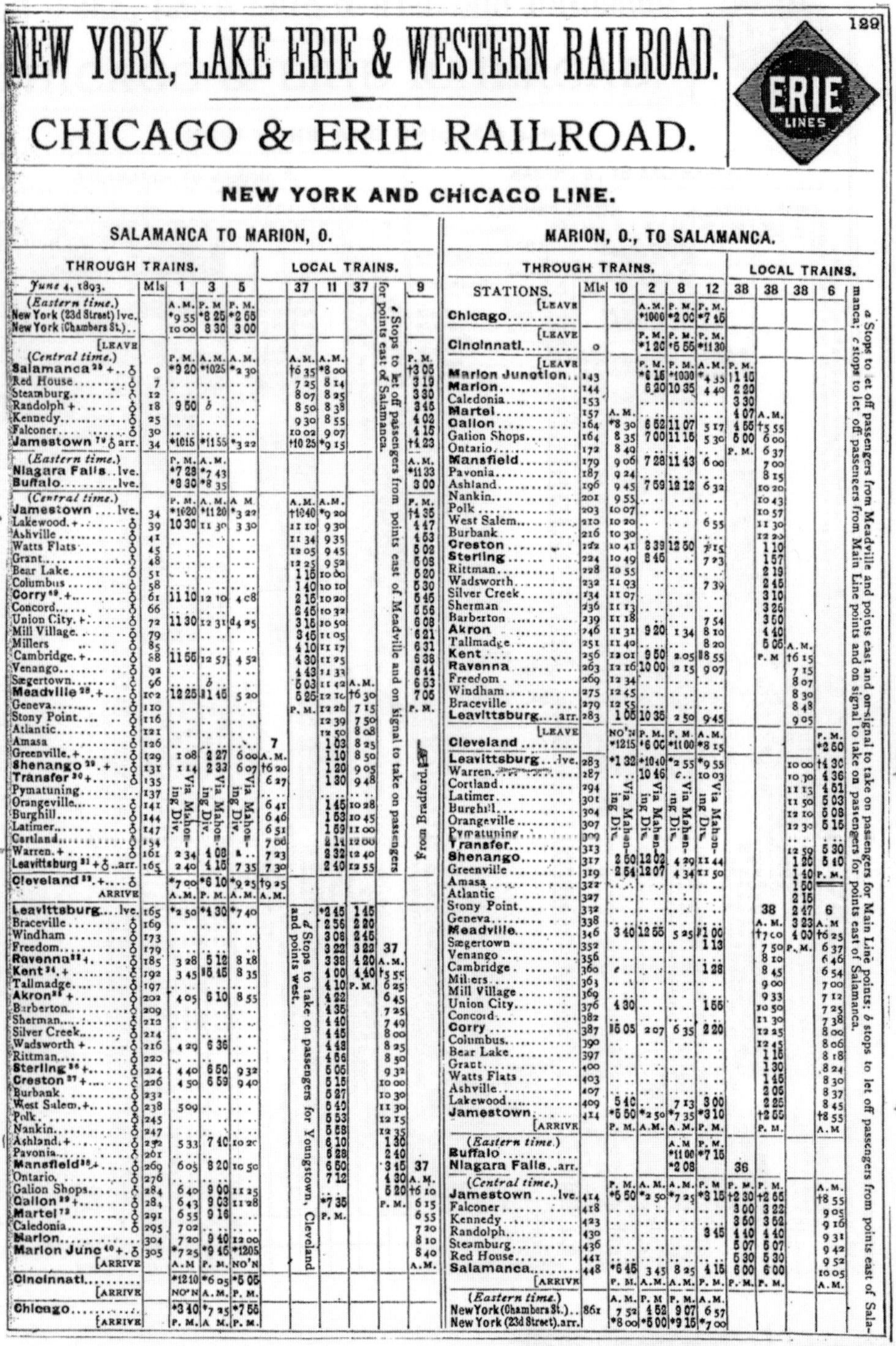

The first known automobile in Lakewood was Ward's Winton. Starting from Warren on August 10, 1899, the car was driven to Lakewood where it was used with much notoriety for several weeks before being returned to Warren by train on September 12.

The first Packard automobile to arrive in Lakewood was driven by Will and WA Hatcher. The journey began in Warren on June 9, 1900 arriving in Lakewood on the 10th. With the self-described "hard-trip" behind them, the machine was quietly returned to Warren via rail freight the next day.

Other visits by automobile would be noted with increasing frequency through these early years, but it would be over a decade until motoring to Lakewood became a common occurrence. Most visible in those pioneering days was Ward and Elizabeth's 1904 honeymoon trek to Lakewood in a Model L Packard.

The Erie Railroad System

Chicago & Erie Railroad – New York & Chicago Line

June 1896 Timetable showing Erie Line with direct service between Leavittsburg / Warren and Lakewood / Jamestown.

The convenience and comforts of travel on the A & GW/ Erie's New York-Chicago line were enjoyed by the Packards for several reasons. Station locations at each end were relatively close to their Warren home (a depot at the corner of Main St. and South St.-about a half mile from their High Street mansion) and to their Lakewood destination (a depot on the corner of 1st St. and Chautauqua Avenue-less than half a mile from the Lakeview Hotel and the adjacent Packard cottages). On the Warren end, it was also possible to alternatively board a train at Leavittsburg if a more convenient one was not scheduled to stop at the Warren depot four miles down the road.

With several major rail lines converging on Warren, almost 60 trains per day were going through town during the railroads' heyday.

City streetcar/interurban service by the Jamestown Street Railway Company was available from the Lakewood depot to the hotels facing Lake Chautauqua. On the Warren end the Trumbull Electric Railroad Company interurban lines also connected some of the city beginning in 1893, but were not directly helpful to the Packard family travels. Ward did invest in this company and was a director of TERR Co. beginning in 1894. The company later added more track within the city of Warren, becoming the Mahoning Valley Railway Co. Their streetcars remained active in Warren until the end of 1931.

Two generations of the Packards of Warren used the A & GW/Erie railroad connections with great frequency, noting arrivals and departures in their diaries. Without the railroads there probably would not have been a Warren-Lakewood connection by the Packards.

Atlantic & Great Western / Erie Passenger Depots

Warren Station
Corner of Main & South Streets
Ca. 1910

Lakewood Station
Corner of 1st Street & Chautauqua Avenue
Ca. 1900

Chapter 9

The Packard Homes at Lakewood/Chautauqua

Warren Packard began construction of his imposing new mansion in Warren during 1874. In that year he also traveled to California to reconnect with a father he hadn't known for 25 years.

1874 was also a year of major investment by Warren in property at Lake Chautauqua. With brother, John R. Packard, Warren acquired an interest in the "Lakeview House" resort hotel in what would become the village of Lakewood, New York. "Lakeview House" had been constructed by John Cowing in 1870. The prospects for favorable resort business were already growing rapidly, in spite of a severe national financial meltdown known as The Panic of 1873.

The Panic had proven to be no impediment to Warren's entrepreneurial dynamic. In spite of substantial losses in his iron forge and rolling mill businesses as well as the disastrous Youngstown hardware store fire, his huge profits in the lumber business made these losses insignificant. He was on a roll.

In addition to the hotel, Warren purchased 25 acres adjoining the hotel site. This became developed as the "Lakeview Tract". Many substantial summer cottages and homes were subsequently located on the property. The land adjacent to the "Lakeview House" became the later site of Will and Ward's "Twin Cottages", and ultimately the location of Ward's 1911-12 Lakewood Mansion.

The "Lakeview House" itself underwent several transitions. It became the rebuilt "Sterlingworth Hotel" in 1889. The hotel was in turn purchased in 1896 by the Lakewood Hotel & Land Co. and became the "Waldmere". Destroyed by fire in 1902 or '03, it was never rebuilt. Prior to Will and Ward building their own cottages, they apparently spent a number of their visits to Lakewood at the Lakeview House/Sterlingworth as well as at the Warren Packard family summer home. By the time the village of Lakewood incorporated in 1893, there were about 600 permanent residents and an additional 1500 summer visitors annually.

The fortunes of both Will and Ward were favorable enough by the second half of the 1890's that they decided to build cottages for themselves on the shore of Lake Chautauqua at Lakewood. These were known as the "Twin Cottages" and were on land immediately west of the Waldmere. These two prominent "cottages" were moved from the lakeshore to locations south of Terrace Street between 1905 and 1910 to make room for Ward and Elizabeth's new summer mansion. Today the "Twin Cottages" remain as well maintained homes by Lakewood residents.

During 1911 construction began on the new 32 room mansion with extensive out-buildings and landscaped gardens. Ward and Elizabeth moved in during July 1912. After Ward's death in 1928, Elizabeth elected to establish her permanent residence here, transferring the Warren home to her niece. She led an active life in Lakewood, with generous financial gifts and service to her adopted community until her death in 1960. The estate has been converted into condominiums.

The last Packard estate to be constructed on Lake Chautauqua was "Packard Manor". This was built by Will 15 miles from Lakewood at the edge of the Chautauqua Institute grounds. Will commissioned the prestigious New York architectural firm of Warren & Wetmore to design his new lake home. This firm was responsible for the design of many grand edifices including The Commodore Hotel in New York, the Mayflower Hotel in Washington, Grand Central Terminal in New York and The Royal Hawaiian Hotel in Honolulu.

Will's palatial estate was completed in 1916 and used by Will and Kitty until his death in 1923. It is still a well maintained private residence. An excellent and detailed article, "Packard Manor", regarding the estate and its history was written by Cindee Mines and is included in a 2008 issue of the National Packard Museum's *Packard Time Machine*.

Map of Center of the Village of Lakewood, New York

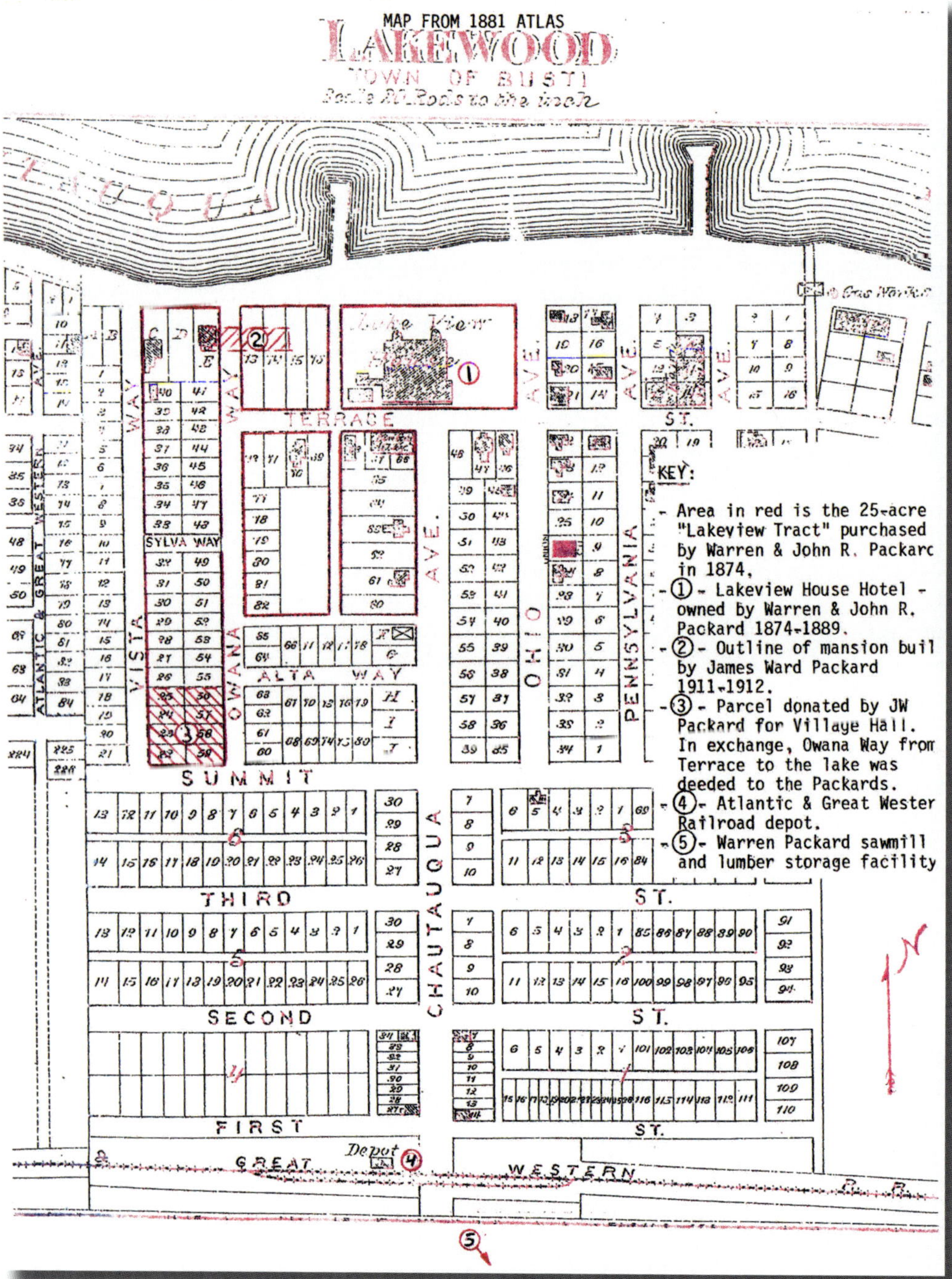

The Sterlingworth Hotel Jamestown Street Railway Car #16 on Chautauqua Avenue, approaching Terrace Street Ca. 1895

View of "Packard Manor" Home of William Doud Packard on Lake Chautauqua Built 1916

"Twin Cottages" — Lakewood, New York

Twin Cottages
Built for William Doud &
James Ward Packard

Twin Cottages
On Lake Chautauqua before they were moved ca. 1905-1910 (Only one cottage is visible in this view)

James Ward Packard Estate at Lakewood, New York

Entrance to Packard estate
Illustrated in 1935 Packard Motor Car Co. advertising brochure, "Famous Packard Gateways"

Chapter 10

Warren Packard — Opportunity and Reward

A dominant characteristic of Warren Packard was his consuming pursuit of opportunity. From his teenage years working for Milton Graham, he developed the courage and acumen to take acceptable business risks. This dynamic, along with honesty and an ability to work well with others, allowed Warren to prosper financially throughout his adult life. The coming of age of railroads in America was another major part of the equation, ultimately bringing great wealth to him.

Starting in the 1850's in the hardware business, Warren soon began developing sources and production of iron hardware items. These ranged from strap iron to forged pieces such as nails, handles and hinges. He partnered with Rolla Barnum in a forge and rolling mill in Warren which was successful for a number of years. However, the demand for basic iron products at the hardware level began declining in the 1870's. The business did not survive.

Warren became the largest wholesale and retail hardware supplier between Cleveland and Pittsburgh. In addition to his Warren, Ohio businesses, he very creatively developed partnerships with brothers Andrew Jackson Packard in Youngstown (W. & A.J. Packard Hardware Co.) and John Randolph Packard in Greenville, Pennsylvania (Packard Hardware Co.). Other partnerships and investments were made in hardware supply companies, real estate and the Lakeview Hotel in Lakewood with brother John Randolph Packard. He also made a major investment in the Austin Flagstone Company, which provided solid dividends for many years.

Will had worked in his father's enterprises, beginning in the 1870's. He was familiar with the many sides of Warren's businesses. By the second half of the 1890's Warren's health was rapidly declining. He began to transfer management of the various businesses to Will, with some directorship positions for Ward and other members of the family.

Warren died in July 1897. It now fell to his oldest son to divest or maintain his various operations and to assure that proper profits or liquidated assets were added to Warren's estate. The decade of the 1890's had been chaotic for Will even before the death of his father. This added responsibility would be an enormous test of his abilities.

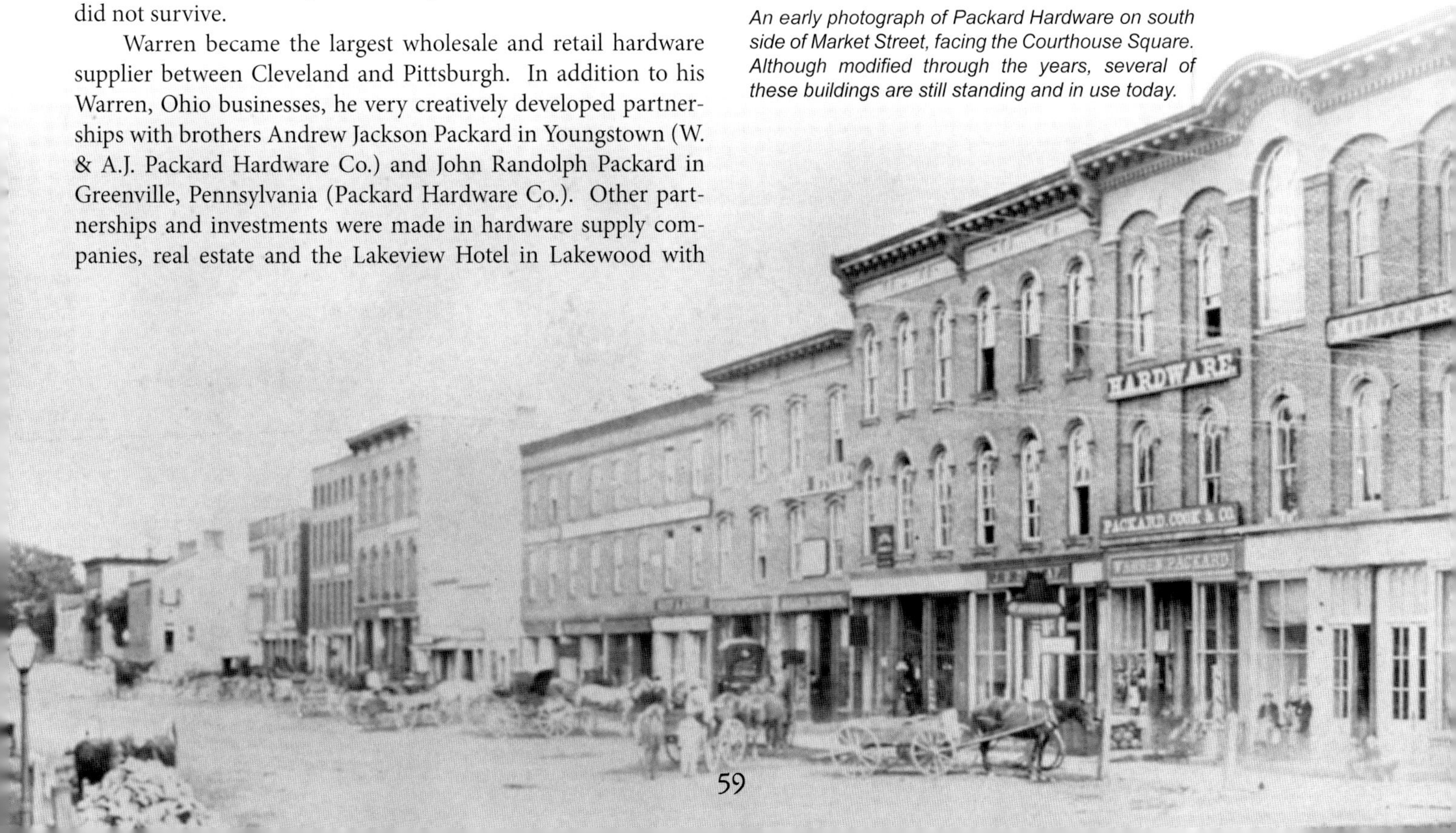

An early photograph of Packard Hardware on south side of Market Street, facing the Courthouse Square. Although modified through the years, several of these buildings are still standing and in use today.

Will did successfully guide his father's businesses, continuing several of them into the 20th century. While several of the businesses had been liquidated or divested, the Packard Hardware Company of Greenville would carry on for almost two decades with Warren's brother John R. as president. The successful Warren Packard Company of Warren, Ohio would supply lumber and shingles well into the 1900's.

Warren Packard's dynamism and entrepreneurial skill had created a major business foundation for the next generation. His sons would develop new enterprises in the maturing Age of Electricity with even greater success.

Some of Warren Packard's Business Letterheads

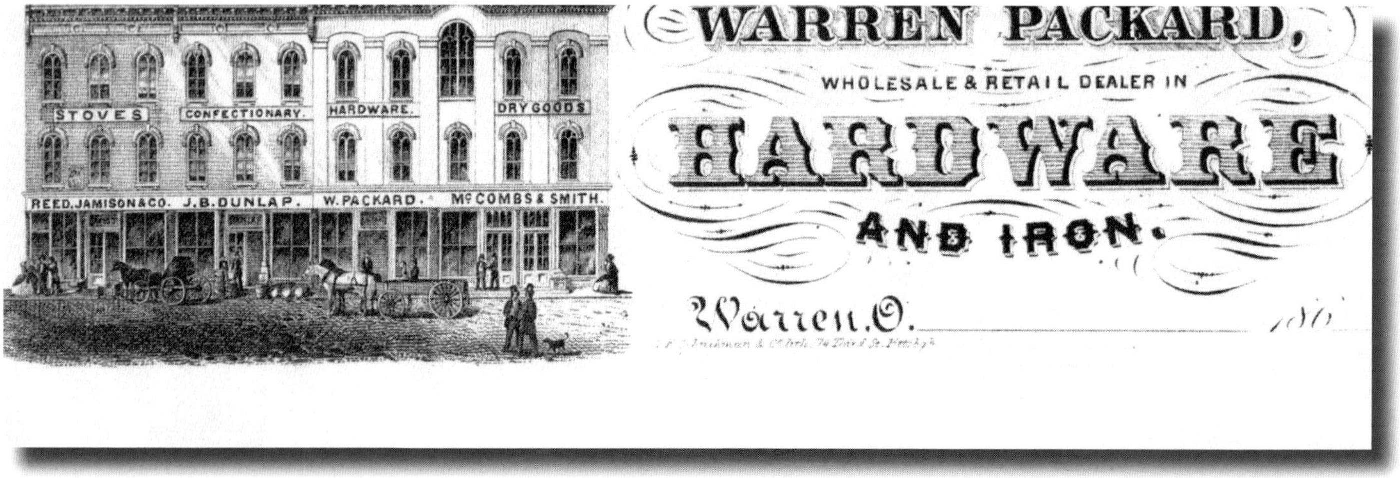

Note the similarity of masthead illustrations on headings of various Warren Packard companies.

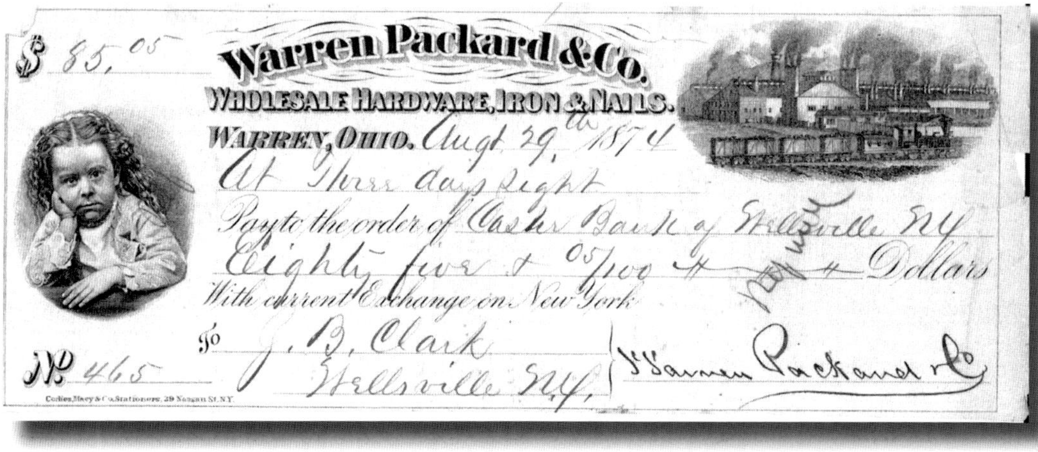

ESTABLISHED 1851.

Babbitt, Brooks & Smith.

WARREN PACKARD & CO.

JOBBERS OF

IRON, HARDWARE & PAINTS.

JOHNS & CO. LITH. CLEVELAND, O.

Warren, O. January 31st 1883.

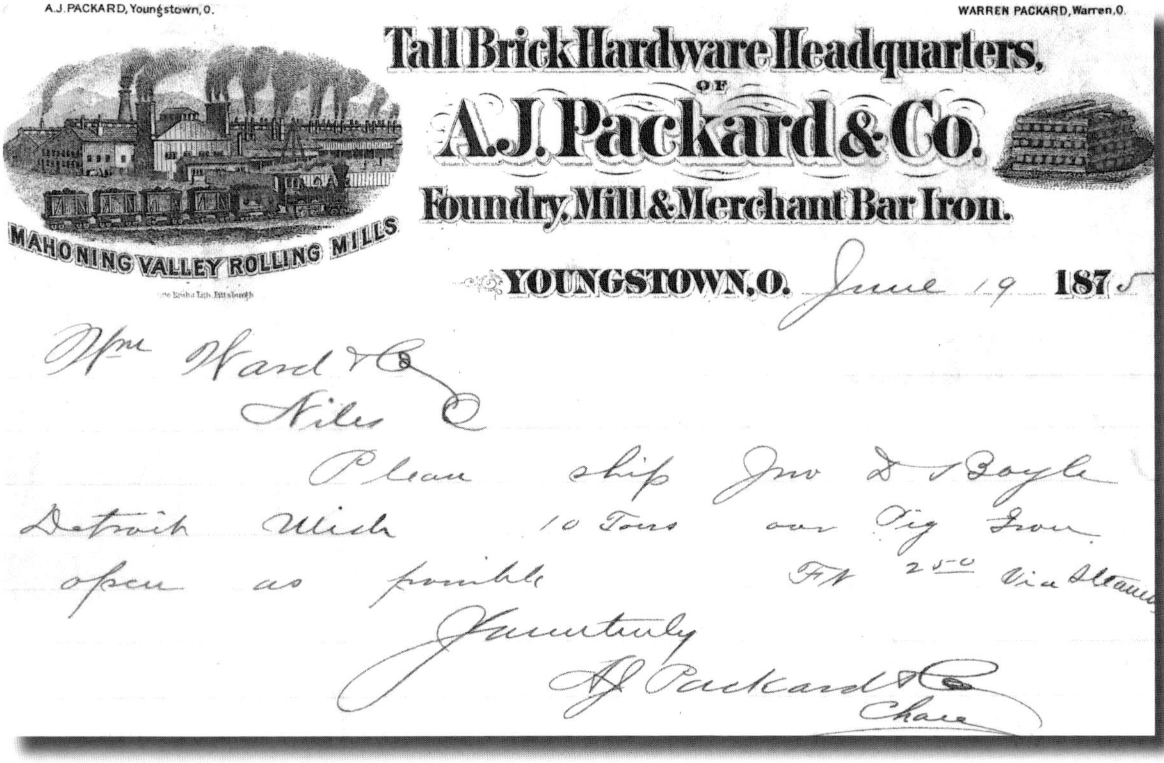
A. J. PACKARD, Youngstown, O.

WARREN PACKARD, Warren, O.

Tall Brick Hardware Headquarters,

OF

A. J. Packard & Co.

Foundry, Mill & Merchant Bar Iron.

YOUNGSTOWN, O. June 19 1875

Wm Ward & Co

Niles O

Please ship Jno D. S. Boyle

Detroit Mich 10 Tons our Pig Iron

soon as possible Ft 2.50 via steamer

Yours truly

A J Packard & Co

Chase

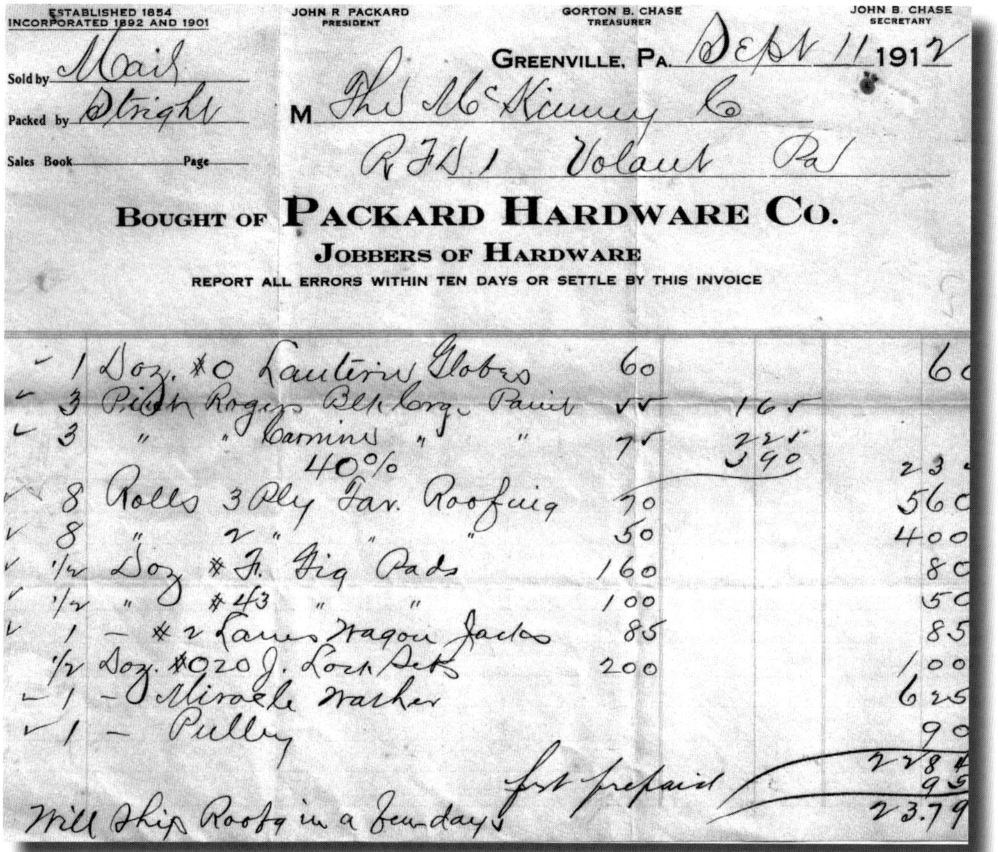

ESTABLISHED 1854
INCORPORATED 1892 AND 1901

JOHN R PACKARD
PRESIDENT

GORTON B. CHASE
TREASURER

JOHN B. CHASE
SECRETARY

Sold by Mail

Packed by Stright

Sales Book ______ Page ______

GREENVILLE, PA. Sept 11 1912

M The McKinney Co
RFD 1 Volant Pa

BOUGHT OF PACKARD HARDWARE CO.

JOBBERS OF HARDWARE

REPORT ALL ERRORS WITHIN TEN DAYS OR SETTLE BY THIS INVOICE

1	Doz. #0 Lantern Globes	60		60
3	Pints Rogers Blk Carg. Paint	55	165	
3	" " Carmine " "	75	225	
	40%		390	234
8	Rolls 3 Ply Tar. Roofing	70		560
8	" 2 " "	50		400
1/2	Doz #F. Fig Pads	160		80
1/2	" #43 " "	100		50
1	– #2 Lanes Wagon Jacks	85		85
1/2	Doz. #020 J. Lock Sets	200		100
1	– Miracle Washer			625
1	– Pulley			90
	frt prepaid			2284
				95
				23.79

Will Ship Roofg in a few days

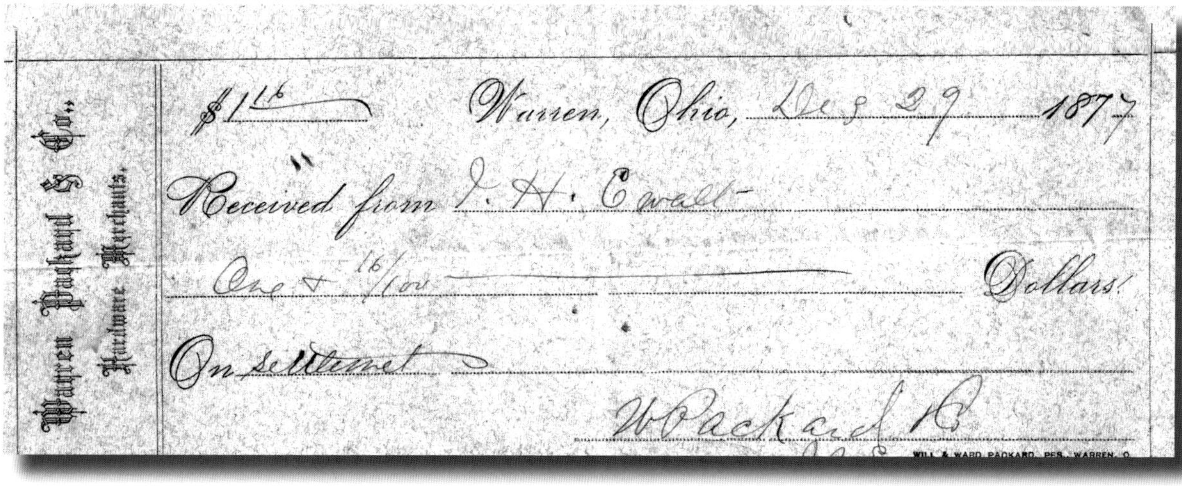

Warren Packard & Co.,
Hardware Merchants.

$1 16/100 Warren, Ohio, Dec 29 1877

Received from J. H. Ewalt

One & 16/100 Dollars.

On settlement

W Packard & Co

WILL & WARD PACKARD, PER. WARREN, O.

The Packard Hardware Co. (Greenville, PA) heading is from 1912-15 years after the death of Warren Packard. In 1912 that company's president was John R. Packard.

Warren Packard's Business Enterprises

— Worked for Milton Graham's Hardware Store, Warren, Ohio from 1846-1851

— Completely owned former Graham Hardware Store by 1851.

— Joined with brother Andrew Jackson Packard In W. & A.J. Packard Hardware Co., Youngstown, Ohio ca. 1860.

— Bought out Harmon Hardware Co., Warren, Ohio in 1863. Now called Packard & Harmon. Also absorbed the store of Thomas Morely.

— Founded the Pacard Co., Lakewood, New York. Property management and a sawmill operation was started in Lakewood.

— Was a major investor in Packard, Hull & Co., and S.L. Abell & Co., suppliers of hardware items. Also a major investor in Austin Flagstone Co.

— Founded Warren Packard Co., a major supplier of lumber to the railroads. Also leased tracts of land in several states and erected temporary sawmills to supply the demand for lumber. Other markets were (plank) roads and roof shingles.

— Joined with Rolla Barnum in Packard & Barnum, South Street, Warren, Ohio. This was a steam forge and rolling mill operation that produced iron parts.

Chapter II

The Packards and the Age of Electricity

Ward had exhibited curiosity and an analytic mind for all things mechanical from an early age. It was natural for him to choose the Mechanical Engineering curriculum at Lehigh University for his residency there beginning in 1880. Throughout his life there was a passion to examine machines and their design. This study reached its zenith with Ward's later collection of timepieces, specifying "complications" for special-order watches that became part of America's premier private timepiece collection.

Ward also recognized the significance of the new Age of Electricity. He is said to have developed an electro-magnetic remote control device for his college dorm room door. His graduation thesis, "Design & Working Drawings for A 4-Light Dynamo Electric Machine" displayed his detailed working knowledge of electricity. As electrical technology unfolded in these early years, Ward was aware of the technical strengths and weaknesses of various electrical theories.

His 1884-1890 employment by Sawyer-Man/Thomson-Huston in New York City, a large supplier of electrical products, set the stage for creation of a major Packard industrial presence in the Age of Electricity and beyond.

With brother Will overseeing the business and sales activities, Ward himself would handle the technical and manufacturing end of a new business based in their hometown of Warren, Ohio. The Packard Electric Company was incorporated in June 1890. It was soon evident that local investors had not raised sufficient capital to get the business running. Subsequent promotion by Ward with his old contacts in New York did bring satisfactory capital, but with the proviso from the new investors that a separate company be formed. The New York and Ohio Co. was thus incorporated in January 1891.

The Packard businesses in Warren were now off and running. In the early years Packard Electric provided the land and buildings for this new venture with the New York and Ohio Co. owning equipment and materials and providing most of the manpower. The two companies were almost wholly symbiotic for most of the 1890's.

During the first decade of the 20th century a distinct division of products and company assets became more evident. The New York & Ohio Co. continued to focus on electrical light bulbs and componentry. In 1904 it became part of the National Electric Lamp Association (NELA). They were acquired by General Electric in 1911 and remained as the Ohio Lamp Plant for General Electric until completely closing down in January 2014.

The Packard Electric Co. evolved as a supplier of electrical componentry to the rapidly growing automobile industry, pioneering products such as wiring looms and insulated cable for vehicles. General Motors Corporation acquired Packard Electric in 1932. For the 21st century Packard Electric was spun off as a parts supply component of the newly created Delphi group, now independent of General Motors.

During the early years, a significant subsidiary of Packard Electric Co. was created in Canada. The full story of this operation is contained in an excellent book, *"Ferranti-Packard / Pioneers in Canadian Electrical Manufacturing"*, by Norman R. Ball and John N. Vardalas.

Another lesser known company in the portfolio of Will and Ward during the mid 1890's was the Packard Enameling Company, located on North Avenue (now Dana Street) east of the Packard Electric properties. Their involvement in this processing company that painted various products for other companies began in September 1894, when the Specialty Wood Working Co. was acquired and reorganized as the Packard Enameling Company. At that time the new company purchased land from Will and Ward for $1,300. The brothers had acquired this land from J.B. Perkins for $900 a month earlier. By July 1896 the equipment and materials from this venture were sold to a West Virginia concern for $3,735. The Packard Enameling Co. land and building were sold to the Packard Electric Co. for needed expansion. The price for this real estate to Packard Electric was $6,000. In December 1896 the Packard Electric Winding Department was moved into the old enameling company building. The Packard Enameling Company remains a little known footnote in Packard history.

The creation of the Packard Electric and New York & Ohio companies in 1890-91, along with the nascent automotive operation started in 1899, provided America with a contribution to economic prosperity unequaled by all but a few organizations. The Packard brothers, Will and Ward, are due much credit for their role in these creations and their further development.

Letterhead of the Packard Enameling Company

Photo of Packard Electric and New York & Ohio Facilities - 1898

The companies' offices were located in the house, the nearest building in this photo. The house was constructed in 1898.

The factory's power plant is hidden between the house and the next building. The power plant was constructed in 1890 as part of the original Packard Electric site.

The original Packard Electric plant building (with peaked roof) was erected in 1890.

The addition to the original Packard Electric plant building (with flat roof) was erected in 1891. The first Packard automobile (1899) was built in this addition.

Letterhead of the Packard Electric Co., Ltd.

Packard Electric Co., Ltd. was a subsidiary of the Packard Electric Co. Note company officers on masthead.

Packard Electric Co. Advertisements — 1907

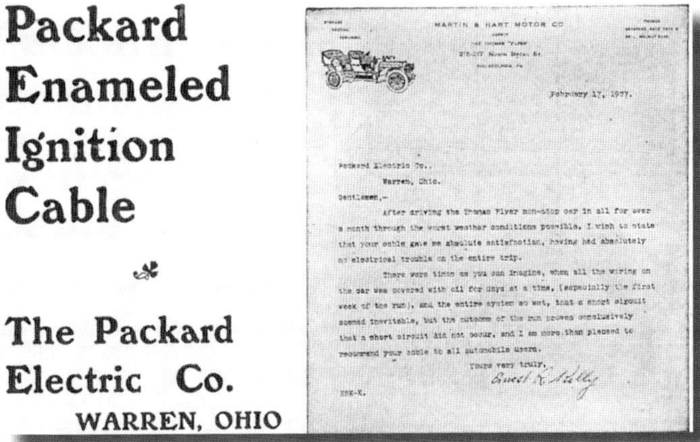

MARTIN & HART MOTOR CO

February 17, 1907.

Packard Electric Co.,

Warren, Ohio.

Gentlemen,-

After driving the Thomas Flyer non-stop car in all for over a month through the worst weather conditions possible, I wish to state that your cable gave me absolute satisfaction, having had absolutely no electrical trouble on the entire trip.

There were times as you can imagine, when all the wiring on the car was covered with oil for days at a time, (especially the first week of the run), and the entire system so wet, that a short circuit seemed inevitable, but the outcome of the run proves conclusively that a short circuit did not occur, and I am more than pleased to recommend your cable to all automobile users.

Yours very truly,

ERK-K.

Letterhead of the New York & Ohio Co.

New York & Ohio Company

J. W. PEALE, Prest.
1 BROADWAY. NEW YORK.
J. W. PACKARD,
Vice Prest and Genl Mgr.
WARREN, OHIO.
W. D. PACKARD,
Secretary and Treasurer.
WARREN, OHIO.

MANUFACTURERS OF
THE Packard INCANDESCENT LAMP AND TRANSFORMER.

BRANCH OFFICES
CHICAGO-92-94 W. VAN BUREN ST.
NEW YORK-1 BROADWAY.

MAIN OFFICE & WORKS,
WARREN, OHIO.

WARREN, OHIO. Nov. 16, 1900

Note officers of the company on masthead.

NOVEMBER, 1908

PRICE LIST

HOLOPHANE REFLECTORS

Packard

INTENSIVE, EXTENSIVE AND FOCUSING TYPES

TUNGSTEN, TANTALUM AND GEM LAMPS

NEW YORK & OHIO COMPANY
WARREN, OHIO

MERIDIAN TUNGSTEN LAMP
WITH S REFLECTOR AND H HOLDER

We do not show light distribution curve of S Reflector.

The distribution is similar to the Intensive Type with downward c. p. of 40 candle for the 40 watt and 80 candle for the 60 watt Meridian Tungsten Lamps. This type of reflector is adapted for all general use.

Chapter 12

The Packard Automobiles of Warren, Ohio

The greatest recognition today of the Packard family is reserved for the automobiles bearing their name. Packards were produced from 1899 through the 1958 model year, although the last two years of the marque consisted only of modified and rebadged Studebakers. Total Packard auto production for all years was near 1.6 million vehicles. Of this total, only about 400 were produced before the company moved to Detroit in October 1903.

It all started with the prototype Packard Model A which first ran in Warren, Ohio on November 6, 1899. This prototype was the culmination of a challenge from Alexander Winton to Ward to build a better auto if he could, after Ward had spent a frustrating year tinkering with his 1898 Winton machine and making many suggestions to Winton regarding possibilities for improving it. The proud Scotsman would end up creating a formidable competitor.

Ward quietly accepted the challenge. In July 1899 he established a partnership known as "Packard & Weiss" to build a prototype machine, with the possibility of extending production if the prototype was successful. The partners and initial investors were Ward, Will, and George Lewis Weiss who had been a major stockholder in Winton's business. Weiss decided to liquidate his holdings with Winton and invest in the new Packard venture. The three partners made a commitment to proceed based upon convincing Winton employee William Hatcher to leave Winton and come to Warren. Hatcher enthusiastically agreed and the partnership became operational that same month.

The full story of Packard automotive history in Warren is well presented in Terry Martin's book, *Packard-The Warren Years*. Commentary herein will focus on the corporate relationships and changes made while Packard auto production remained in Warren.

The original Packard & Weiss partners agreed to initially invest $3,000 each in the project. Model A Number 1 was built in the Packard Electric shops while the materials, tools, and manpower were billed to the partnership through the New York & Ohio Co.

The Packard auto was well received. It was quickly decided to proceed with the first lot of vehicles. The second car built (A-21) was used by Will and the third (A-22) was sent to Cleveland for George Weiss' personal use and demonstrations. By May 1900 the first cars for sale to customers were being delivered. By June the Model B was in production. Clearly, expansion of the automobile business was in the cards. Continuous demands for working capital to accommodate increased production meant that the original partnership had to be reassessed.

The answer was to incorporate the new automobile business, with provisions to increase its capitalization. The result was creation of the Ohio Automobile Co. (OAC) incorporated in the state of West Virginia on September 10, 1900. Ward, Will, and George Weiss remained the major stockholders. Provisions were included in OAC's charter to allow capitalization up to $500,000. Ward was named president, George Weiss was vice president, and Will was secretary/treasurer.

The OAC then acquired the new 1899 Packard Electric building. The materials, tools, and equipment used in auto production were purchased from the New York & Ohio Co. The Packard automobile business would now stand alone.

By October 1901, 760 shares of OAC stock ($100 par value) had been distributed, with most of it going to the original partners.

New investors from Detroit, led by Henry Bourne Joy, began to make major investments in the fledgling company during 1902. At the stockholder's meeting on October 13, 1902 the corporate name was changed to the Packard Motor Car Co. The company remained incorporated in West Virginia and would not become a Michigan corporation until 1909, six years after the factory's move to Detroit. After that October meeting the Detroit Free Press newspaper reported that "the company had been acquired by Detroit investors". The factory would be moved from Warren to Detroit as soon as feasible. Although the Packard Motor Car Co. retained Ward as president, George Weiss as vice president and Will as secretary/treasurer, the equation would change a month later when Henry B. Joy replaced Weiss as vice president.

Control of the company's fortunes had now passed from the original three partners to a group of Detroit investors headed by Henry Joy. Despite Ward's denials in Warren, the company's move to Detroit was only a year away.

In the meantime two additional buildings would expand the Packard factory in Warren. First was a frame two-story building added during 1902, then a brick two-story building erected in 1903 between the original OAC building and the 1902 structure.

But the die had been cast. On May 11 Packard's Board of Directors approved the purchase of six acres of land on East Grand Boulevard in Detroit at $3,000 an acre. The sale of that parcel from the old Beaufait Farm was recorded on June 8, 1903 by the Wayne County recorder and included 6.478 acres "more or less".

As events unfolded, Joy was obviously in charge. Although always deferential to Ward, Joy's dynamism quickly established his leadership initiative. Ward remained as president long after the move to Detroit but his role was essentially ceremonial after 1903.

While Will and Ward had both retained significant stock holdings in the Packard Motor Car Co., they did not continue any operating participation. Will had relinquished his directorship that October. Ward remained as a director and as president after the move. He would continue to attend board meetings in Detroit. He was elected chairman of the board of Packard, another honorary position, in October 1908. The chairman's position was eliminated by the board in 1912. He finally resigned his directorship in 1915.

Contact with the Packard Motor Car Co. continued to be cordial until Ward's death. He maintained a business friendship with Henry Joy and others in the company. There is correspondence indicating his involvement in acquiring competitor's vehicles for Packard's engineering evaluation in Detroit as late as the 1920's.

The automotive company founded by the Packard brothers would owe its success and prestige to three presidents of the Packard Motor Car Company: James Ward Packard, Henry Bourne Joy and James Alvan Macauley.

Letterhead of the Ohio Automobile Company

Producers of the Packard automobile from September 1900 until October 1902. Note officers of the company on masthead.

Letterhead of the Packard Motor Car Company (Warren)

Producers of the Packard automobile from October 1902 until October 1903. Some PMCCo-Warren letterhead names officers on the masthead.

Model A
1 cylinder

Packard Model A Number 1, parked next to the Packard Electric factory building. Members of the March family – a Packard employee on board in late 1899.

Model B

1 cylinder

Packard No. 30, sold to George Blackmore in August, 1900. Now owned by Terry Martin.

Model C
1 cylinder

Ward in his new 1901 Model C, August 1900.

Model E
1 cylinder

Packard No. 71, a special built for Ward.
Only (1) "E" was built.

1902 Model F

1 cylinder

New York Auto Show car.

1903 Model F
1 cylinder

Early version shown, with gasoline and oil tank fill caps protruding through the cowl.
Improvement for 1903 included a longer wheelbase and body refinements.

Model G

2 cylinders

A very massive machine.

Model K

4 cylinders

Packard recalled the Model K, due to excessive mechanical problems.
"The car that Henry Joy loved to hate."

Model M

2 cylinders

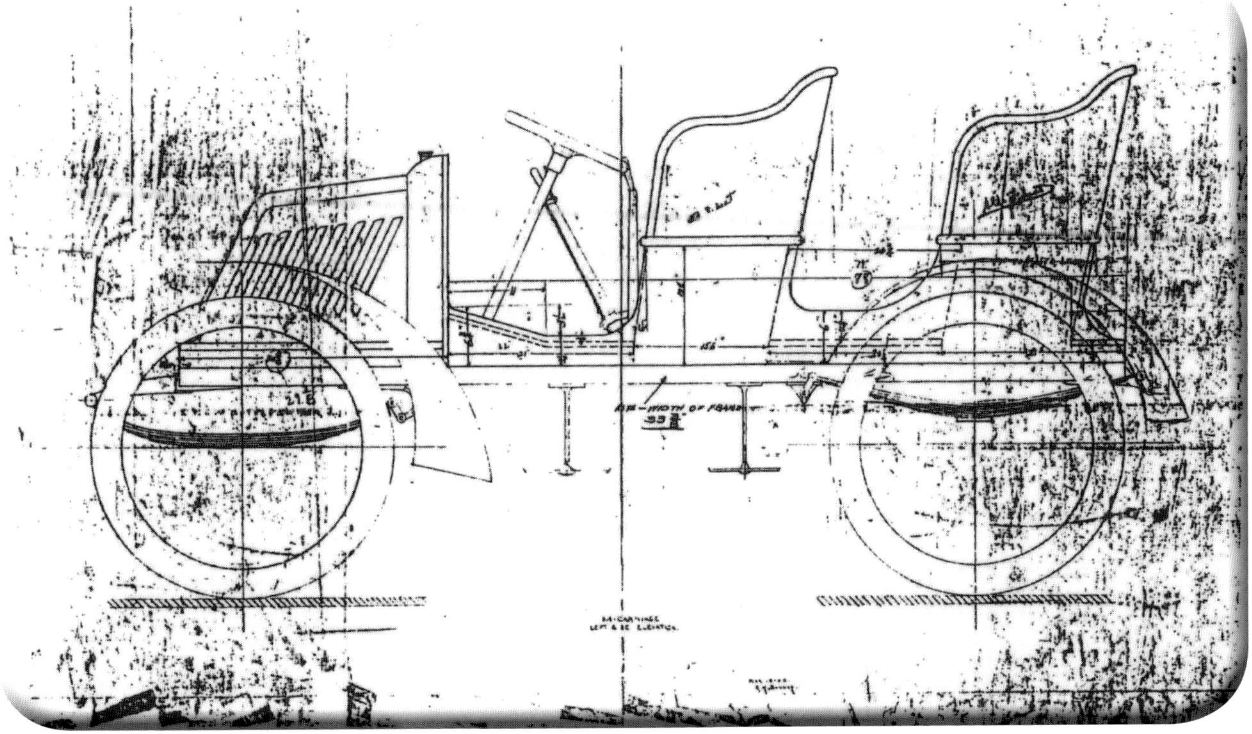

(1) Prototype built, tests were very disappointing, and development was stopped in June 1903.
No photographs of the model are known to exist.

Chapter 13

Hobbies and Interests

Horses and Dogs

Nineteenth century Americans relied on horses for a wide range of labor tasks, including the motive power for transportation in several forms. It wasn't until the development of the automobile in the 20th century that Old Dobbin would be retired from the business of human transportation.

The Packard family of the 19th century also owned horses. Diary entries provided insight into their value to the family for transportation and for pleasure. Several entries disclosed emotional attachments.

The family horse "Grover" was sold by Ward to Al's new husband, E.B. McCrum in 1894 for $50. Was it a coincidence that the horse carried the same name as contemporary President Grover Cleveland, a Democrat? The Packard family was staunch Republican. Cleveland's second term, just starting, was highly politically charged. Perhaps the name "Grover" was a statement being made.

We don't know if it was "Grover" who was the unfortunate victim of an altercation with a locomotive in 1901 as recorded in Will's diary: "Al's horse ran away and was killed by train #12-buggy completely wrecked." It was November 3, Will's 40th birthday.

Another member of the Packard equine family had met a tragic end during January 1899. "Cupid", a Packard family horse born in 1872, was killed under murky circumstances while being boarded for the winter at the farm of William Oliver in Braceville. According to Mary Packard's diary, "Carlotta and Olive cried themselves sick over it."

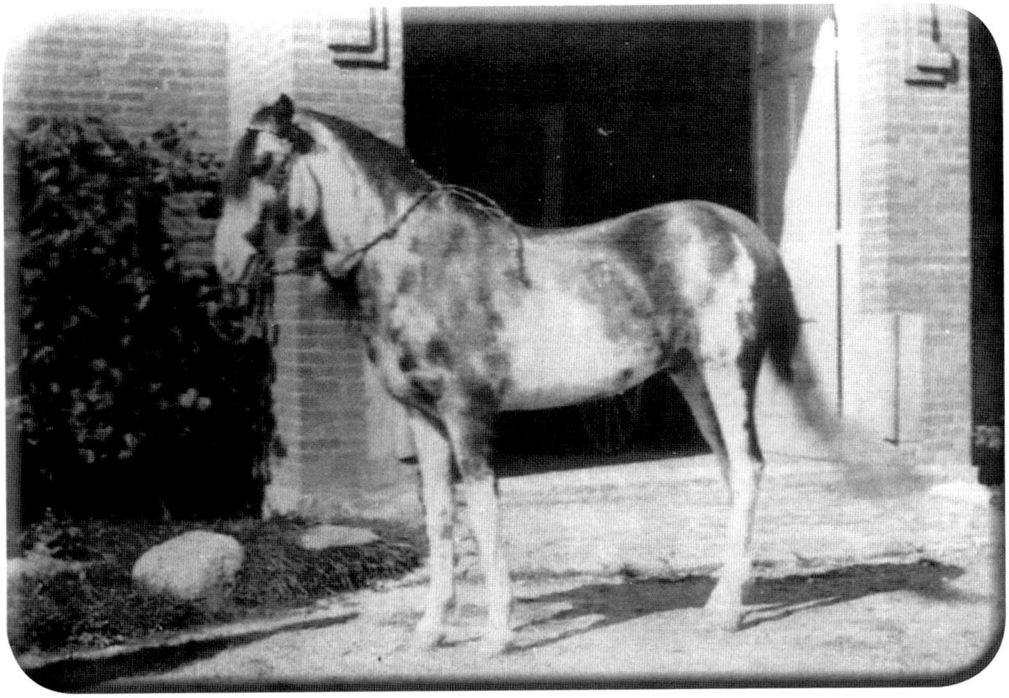

"Cupid" the Packard pony in front of the family's carriage house, behind the mansion at #2 High Street

Packard Model A Number One, parked on Courthouse Square, with "Towser" and "Fritz" in front.
This photo is from the Wendell F. Lauth collection

But it was the family dogs that always remained the favored pets of the Packard siblings. All three of the girls had deep involvements with canine companions. In addition to the recorded family travels to and from Lakewood with dogs in tow as part of the retinue, the girls all had unique relationships with their dogs long after leaving Warren.

Alaska continued to breed and raise dogs at her Independence Lodge home in Virginia. Her will instructed her estate's executor, brother-in-law Guy Gardner, to destroy all remaining dogs in her care after her death. According to the estate's final billing reconciliation, this was done according to her wishes.

Carlotta pampered her beloved dog "Chico" to the end while living in her luxury New York City high rise. She attained some degree of notoriety in September 1938 when she was ticketed and fined $5 by New York City Court for walking Chico through Central Park without a muzzle. The event deeply upset Carlotta and was reported in detail in New York City newspapers.

Olive was apparently also fond of dogs after her move to Cleveland. She was credited in the local newspapers as the first in Cleveland to own poodles, having obtained hers from a kennel in Boston.

The dogs mentioned by both Will and Ward in their diaries through the years were numerous. Perhaps "Towser" obtained the most notoriety throughout his life (ca 1895 to 1908), but there were others.

Ward's diary entry for August 31, 1894 read, "Mother, Olive, Bess G and Finch returned to Warren on #3". "Finch" was the family's dog and, ironically, this first known mention of Elizabeth Gillmer (Bess G.) by Ward in his diaries was exactly ten years to the day before his marriage to her.

Finch's death a few weeks after the return from Lakewood was also noted in Ward's diary. Less than a year later Ward had purchased "Mike" from the Cleveland Kennel Club for $35 (about $950 in today's dollars) at about the same time Carlotta acquired Towser.

Around the turn of the century two additional canines were recorded as members of the family. "Fritz", a dachshund, appeared to be a devoted companion with Towser.

"Joe" was first recorded in Ward's diary on April 13, 1901: "Turned Joe over to E.G." (Elizabeth Gillmer). On May 5, 1901 Ward again made an entry in his diary, "Dog Joe" got caught in chain under carriage. Badly chewed up."

Joe gained recognition in another way, as described in a letter to Ward written by an old business acquaintance as Ward lay dying of cancer on January 24, 1928: "I was starting Motor World (an automotive trade journal) when I went to Warren to your factory and enquired for you. I was told you were out in the plant and invited to await you in your office. I entered through a swinging black leather covered door which was brass studded. If I remember rightly, there was a fireplace, and a dog – an Airedale – was lying on the rug. I did not venture to get familiar with him or to approach him but sat at some distance with my back to the door. I started to talk quietly with him whereupon he first cocked one ear enquiringly, then raised his head and after some time slowly arose, yawned and stretched, then came over toward me and rested his muzzle on my crossed hands. Hearing a slight noise, I turned with some embarrassment to find you with a wide grin watching the performance. Your first words were 'I don't know who you are, but if you are good enough for my dog, you're good enough for me.' We got talking dogs and you told me of this chap's trick in running in front of your automobile, encouraging the other dogs to follow him, then jumping to one side with the hope that some of the others would be run over. All this may have passed completely from your mind and been submerged with the pressure of weightier affairs of today, but it has never left mine. Memories remain and I hope I may be pardoned for reminiscing at this length."

Joe the Airedale probably decided to retire from car chasing after the 1901 incident.

Bicycles

Bicycling was very popular in the 1880s and beyond. By the early 1890s there had been an evolution from high-wheelers to bikes with equal-size wheels, and chain or shaft drives for many designs. These changes made bicycle riding much easier and more stable.

Will was an avid biker into his 40s. There are numerous mentions in Packard family diaries of long-distance rides, some of (20) miles or more. Will was accompanied at times by siblings Ward and Carlotta.

Will posing with a high-wheel bicycle, ca. 1880

Ward with his British Royal Enfield motorcycle, ca. 1914-16. Photo was taken near the front entrance to Thumm's Bicycle Shop on West Market Street, which remains almost unchanged to this day. Thumm's was founded in 1909 by Augie Thumm, grandfather of the current owner of the business.

August Thumm relates the story, told by his grandfather, of how Ward attempted to order a custom Harley-Davidson motorcycle, with scaled-down dimensions to match his short stature. When Harley-Davidson declined the project, Ward turned his interest to a specialized Royal Enfield. The finished motorcycle had been dimensionally proportioned to Ward's specifications, and it is thought that (2) such machines were delivered to him through Thumm's shop.

Ward aims at the target in shooting competition at the National Electric Lamp Association (NELA) Conference, July 1905.

From Civil War muskets to contemporary Smith & Wesson presentation pistols, Ward was an avid collector of firearms. And he was known as a reputable marksman.

Ward in his steam launch on Lake Chautauqua, in the 1890s

From his earliest days in Lakewood Ward had a great love for Lake Chautauqua. By the early 1890s he was acquiring boats powered by steam or internal combustion engines – through the years he owned several. Although some were sold, his collection grew.

In February 1892 he acquired a 25-foot launch with a 9 HP naptha (internal combustion) engine. It cost Ward $1094.50 (over $30,000 in today's money), according to his diary entry. By December 1900 he had another launch, purchased from the S.S. & I. Boat Company. And in March 1902 he purchased a larger boat, 35' 4" long according to his diary.

This latter craft may have been the "Arrogant Ark" (aka "Argonaut Ark"), which was recorded as being used in Canadian waters, as well as in Lake Chautauqua. An active member of the Lakewood Yacht Club, at least one of Ward's boats – named the "Carlotta" – survives in Lakewood to this day.

Perhaps Ward's most consuming mechanical interest during the 20th Century was with watches and their inner workings. His interest was so great that after his death his collection of timepieces was for a period of time considered to be the finest in America. During his life, however, Ward's inherent shyness and tendency to shun attention of himself meant that few people were aware of the superb group of watches that he had collected.

The mechanical challenge of timepiece collecting for Ward focused on quality and the combination of "complications" that a given watch would contain. "Complications" refer to the added functions that the watch could perform over and above the normal keeping of time. Chimes, stop watch functions, songs, calendar day displays (some keeping track of leap year through many decades), and even celestial movements were all challenges specified by Ward and executed by watchmakers. Added to the challenge of "complications" was the implied desire to keep the finished timepiece small in size.

Although Will and Ward had presented their father Warren with a fine pocket watch during the 1870's, Ward's first watch obtained as a collector's piece appears to have been obtained in 1903. His collection continued to grow until his death in 1928. The collection ultimately contained over 100 quality timepieces.

Upon Ward's death in 1928, the nucleus of his collection, the finest 31 pieces he had amassed, soon became the property of the Horological Institute of America. The remainder of the pieces stayed in private hands, primarily with members of the family.

The Horological Institute attempted through the years to attract donors to fund a "Temple of Time" which would house their substantial collections. They conducted several showings and exhibits of the Packard watch collection, but in the end the dream of a permanent repository for the institute's collections did not materialize. The watches from the Packard group now reside in collections in Asia and Europe as well as America.

The masterpiece of Ward's collection was a Patek Philippe (Geneva) pocket watch commissioned by him in 1922, costing $16,000 and requiring five years to design and produce. Sadly, it was only delivered to Ward while he remained hospitalized, a few months before his death. This watch, known in collecting circles as "The Packard", was reacquired by Patel Philippe in September 1988 for the sum of $1.3 million – a record at that time. Since them other Packard-owned timepieces have been sold. A Vacheron Constantin pocket watch from the collection garnered $1.8 million at a Christie's auction in June 2011.

The full story of Ward's interest in watches is presented in Stacy Perman's 2013 book, A Grand Complication, which is very thorough with regard to documenting Ward's watch collecting activities.

Inscribed under celestial moving chart is, "Calculated for Warren, Ohio, 42 Degrees, 20 minutes. No. 198023. Made for J.W. Packard, Warren, Ohio, by Patek Phillipe & Co., Geneva, Switzerland, 1922."

THE PACKARD WATCH COLLECTION

Owned by

HOROLOGICAL INSTITUTE OF AMERICA

PAUL MOORE, *Executive Secretary*

PRESENTED AS A COMPLETE EXHIBIT AT THE FOURTH ANNUAL JEWELRY SHOW, AUGUST FIFTH TO NINTH, NINETEEN HUNDRED AND TWENTY-NINE, AT CHICAGO, ILLINOIS, THROUGH THE COURTESY OF THE WEBB C. BALL WATCH COMPANY, CLEVELAND, OHIO.

Horological Institute of America program for display of (30) watches from the Packard collection in Chicago, 5-9 August 1929.

Horological Institute of America booklet of (31) Packard watches from the Packard collection, which were on display at the Chicago Science Museum. Booklet published 1959.

Memberships

The Packard family was involved with many organizations through the years. Mary Doud Packard was a devout member of Christ Episcopal Church in Warren throughout her life. Elizabeth Gillmer Packard also attended Christ Church while living in Warren and it appears that Carlotta regularly attended there during her youth. Surprisingly, the other members of the Packard family in Warren did not seem particularly attentive to religious affiliation.

Mary also joined the Political Equality Club of Warren, as well as the German Club.

Warren, Will and Ward were all long-time active members of the Masonic Order, being affiliated with the Old Erie Lodge No. 3-F & AM in Warren. Will advanced to the rank of 32nd degree Mason. He also participated in the Warren Commandery of Knights Templar.

Both Will and Ward were members of the Franklin Club of Warren, which appears to have emulated a gathering founded in 1727 by Benjamin Franklin of Philadelphia. The original Philadelphia group's charter outlined their desire "to discuss morals, politics and natural philosophy in a spirit of inquiry to improve selves and community".

Ward was elected president of the Warren Franklin Club at their annual meeting in January 1894. On April 17, 1897 Will's diary noted, "Last night first night of Franklin Club in new quarters in Packard Block". There are still today several localities that maintain a Franklin Club based on the original Philadelphia group's charter.

Warren and Ward were known to be members of Warren Lodge No. 295-Benevolent Protective Order of Elk (BPOE). Ironically, the Packard mansion on High Street would serve as home for Elks Lodge 295 in later years.

Although not well known for active social involvements, Ward did also have memberships through the years in the Engineer's Club of New York, Union Club of Cleveland (with wife Elizabeth Gillmer Packard), Detroit Club, Lakewood Yacht Club, and as a founder of the Bicycling Club of Lehigh University. With brother Will and sister Alaska McCrum, he also was a member of the Warren Golf Club early in the 20th century.

Will was known to frequently attend Masonic meetings while on the road for business. From time to time he also would attend evening meetings in various cities of the Concatenated Order of Hoo-Hoo, a fraternal and service organization whose members are associated with the forest products industry. Will's affiliation was via father Warren's lumber milling and sales operations.

Founded in 1892, Hoo-Hoo's exist to this day with chapters in the U.S. and several foreign countries. The stated aim of the Hoo-Hoo is "to foster the health, happiness and long life of its members".

1901 issue of booklet published by the Concatenated Order of Hoo-Hoo, containing a list indicating Will's membership in the organization. Will's diaries note the times he would attend a Hoo-Hoo meeting in the evening, while traveling to major cities on business.

Chapter 14

Philanthropy and Memorials

The dawn of the 20th century found America transformed by the Industrial Revolution. The capitalists and entrepreneurs that had changed the fabric of the country for the better would today be called "the one percent," referring to their great wealth and our federal government's continuing desire to confiscate that wealth to fund their own priorities.

But in those days before the advent of excessive regulation and taxation at all levels, it was the capitalists and entrepreneurs themselves that led a wave of philanthropic largesse. Andrew Carnegie, the man who created a mighty American steel empire, remains well known to this day for his generous and highly visible library funding throughout the country. Other captains of industry and finance funded other interests. The Packard family also made significant contributions to society in several important ways.

Greater wealth accumulation began with Warren Packard's enterprises, especially due to the great demands for lumber by the railroads during their period of rapid expansion after the Civil War.

The most significant generators of wealth for the Packard family came from the Age of Electricity and the investments they would make as a result of their very successful electrical businesses.

This accumulation of wealth would be accompanied by providing employment and a resulting comfortable and improved standard of living for many tens of thousands of employees and their families for over a century-a major accomplishment in itself. But through the years the Packard family also donated generously to their community and to causes they deemed worthy and beneficial to mankind.

Indeed, the philanthropic benefits of the Packards continue to this day. The full accounting of gifts from the Packard estate was not made until after the death of Elizabeth Gillmer Packard in 1960 when final distributions from Ward's estate would be probated.

Many generous gifts to various causes were recognized and honored by the recipients. Some of the tablets or other means of recognition are included herein. There are surely additional public testimonials to their generosity. It is not the intent of this story to chronicle or catalogue the financial details of these gifts.

It is a grateful mirror to the contributions of the Packard family of Warren, Ohio when viewing the number of memorials that have been made to them by others.

LAND DONATED BY
W. D. PACKARD
January 1911

COMMISSIONERS
W.D. Packard, Chairman
A.I. Powers
H. Q. Stiles
J. X. Wadsworth
Auditor - Wm. E. Dilley
Superintendent - R.C. Jones

The W.D. Packard Music Hall

Included in Will's1920 Last Will & Testament were provisions to build a music hall on property included in Packard Park. Due to the premature death of his son Warren II in 1929 and some resulting challenge to the estate distribution, funds for construction were delayed pending judicial review and decision. The hall was finally built in 1955.

Also included in the will was a provision to endow the W.D. Packard Band, which performs to this day.

Leaded Glass Windows Donated to Christ Episcopal Church — Warren, Ohio

Designed by Gorham, these windows were donated by the Packard children in memory of their mother, Mary Elizabeth Doud Packard, in 1911.

Tablet Installed in the Lobby of the Packard Motor Car Company, Detroit, 1927

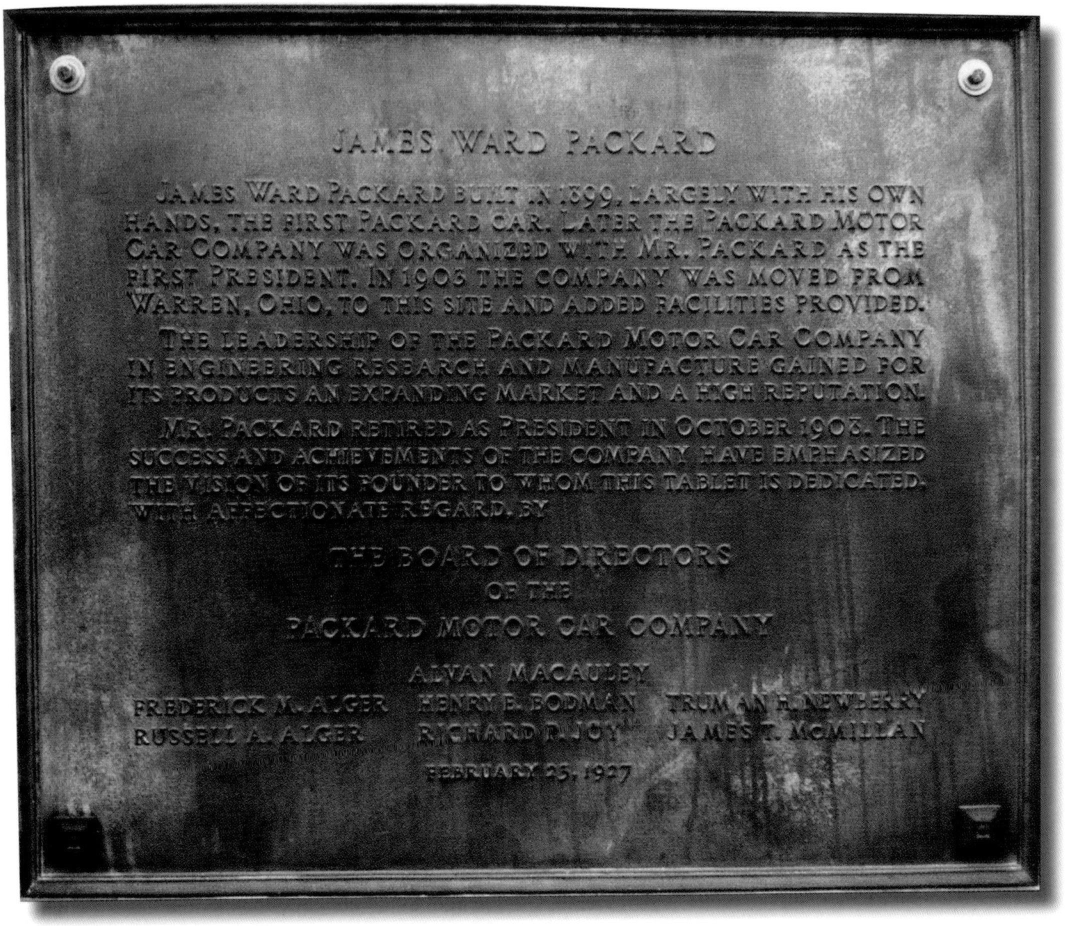

James Ward Packard built in 1899 with his own hands, the first Packard car. Later the Packard Motor Car Company was organized with Mr. Packard as the first president. In 1903 the company was moved from Warren, Ohio to this site and added facilities provided.

The leadership of the Packard Motor Car Company in engineering research and manufacturing gained for its products an expanding market and a high reputation.

Mr. Packard retired as president in October 1908. The success and achievements of the company have emphasized the vision of the founder to which this tablet is dedicated. With affectionate regard, by The Board of Directors Of The Packard Motor Car Company

Alvan Macauley

Frederick M. Alger	*Henry E. Bodman*	*Truman H. Newberry*
Russell A. Alger	*Richard P. Joy*	*James Y. McMillan*

February 23 1927

(Now located at the Packard Proving Grounds, Utica, Michigan)

Tablet Installed by The Salvation Army, Warren, Ohio

THIS
TEMPLE
OF SERVICE TO GOD AND MAN
PERPETUALLY RECALLS THE VISION AND GENEROSITY
of
JAMES W. PACKARD
WARREN, OHIO
1926

Tablet Installed on Public Library, Warren, Ohio

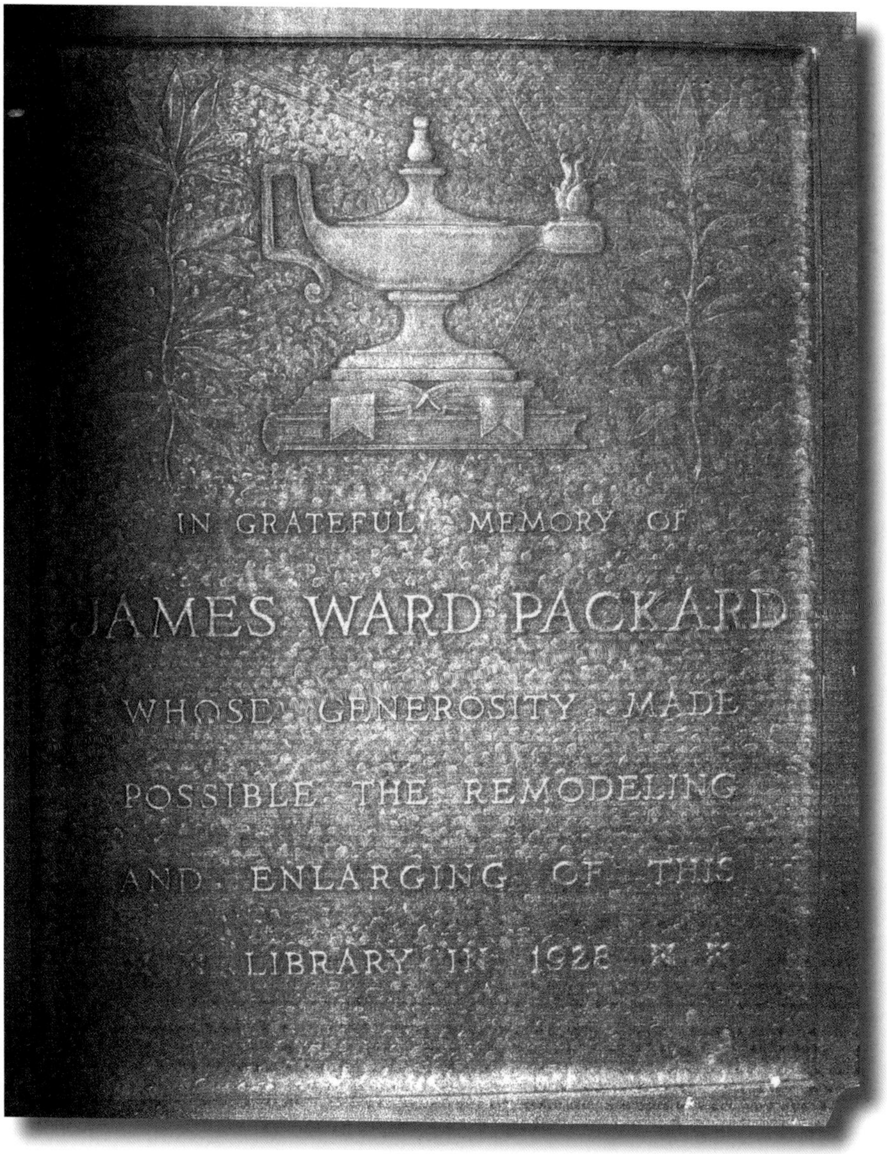

IN GRATEFUL MEMORY OF JAMES WARD PACKARD

WHOSE GENEROSITY MADE POSSIBLE THE REMODELING AND ENLARGEMENT OF THIS LIBRARY IN 1928

Tablet Installed On James Ward Packard Laboratory Of Electrical And Mechanical Engineering

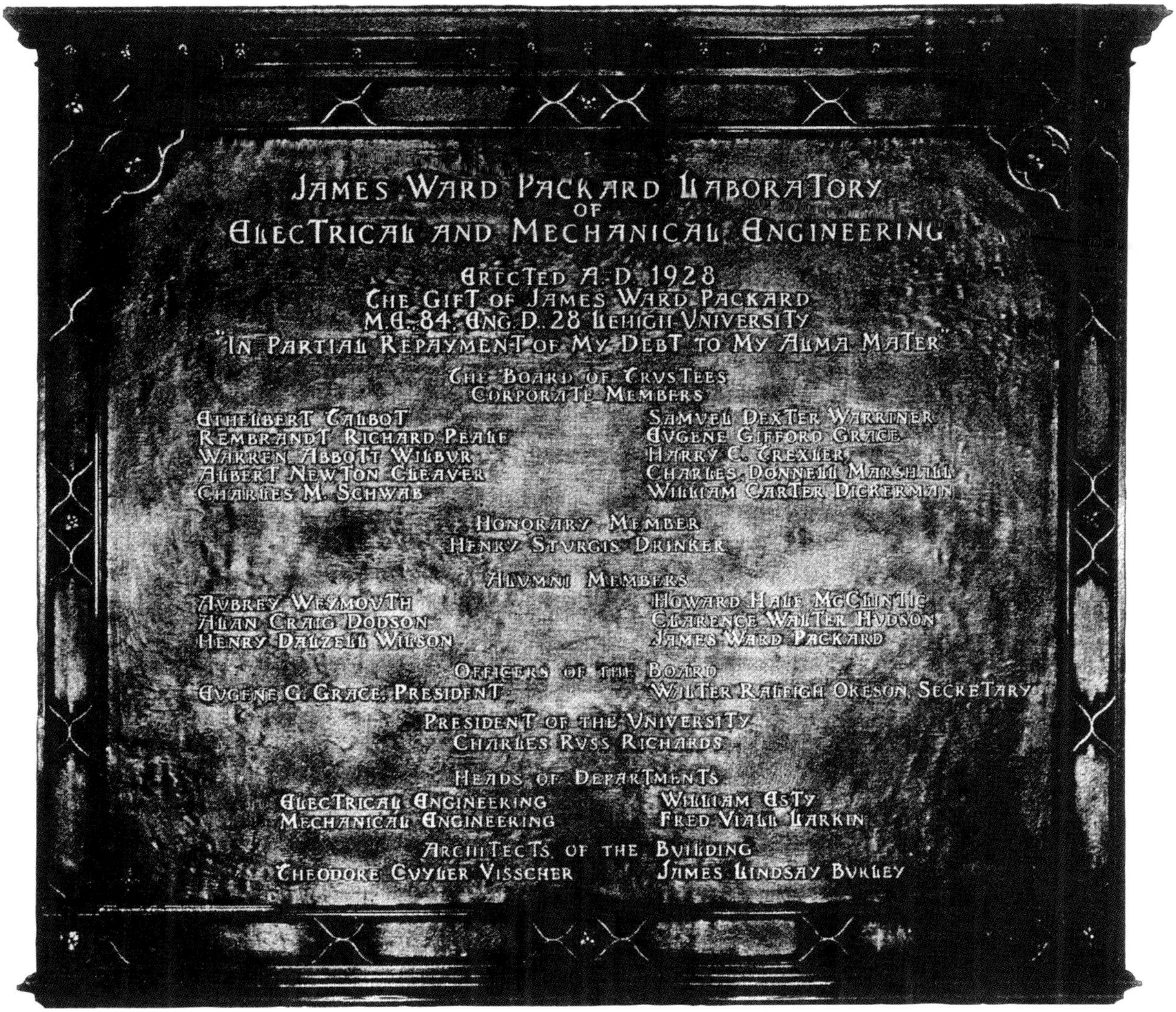

JAMES WARD PACKARD LABORATORY
of
ELECTRICAL AND MECHANICAL ENGINEERING
ERECTED A.D. 1928
The Gift of James Ward Packard M.E. ‘84 D, ‘28 LEHIGH UNIVERSITY

“IN PARTIAL REPAYMENT OF MY DEBT TO MY ALMA MATER”

November 1926 Tribute to Ward by Seaman's Church Institute of New York

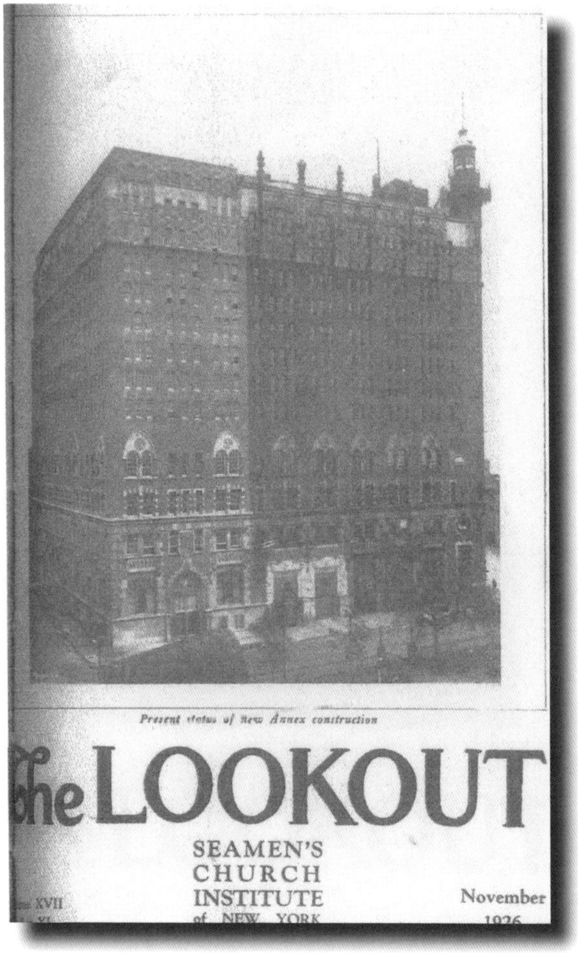

THE LOOKOUT

Another Unconditional Gift

In James Ward Packard, designer of the Packard motor, the Institute has a good friend and a great one. He has long been interested in the mission's aims and services.

When the Institute appealed for $1,500,000 to complete the $2,750,000 fund needed for the new thirteen-story annex, it found that Mr. Packard was also a staunch friend and supporter. He gave $115,000 to the building fund without condition.

At the outset of the campaign, the motor inventor sent a check for $10,000.

Last month, a relative of Mr. Packard visited the building, the Superintendent and officers of the Board of Managers. A few days later the Treasurer received another contribution from the inventor. It was the sum of $105,000.

Mr. Packard expressed his tremendous admiration for the work of the Institute in sheltering, feeding and caring for the seaman. He indicated that his enthusiasm for the mission's work is such that he intends to contribute to its endowment fund.

Announcement of Mr. Packard's $115,000 gift, which was unconditional, closely followed that of John D. Rockefeller, Jr.'s. The sum of $250,000 was given by Mr. Rockefeller.

The gifts of Mr. Packard and Mr. Rockefeller stand as a challenge to New Yorkers of affluence who seek a means of benefiting the less fortunate in worldly goods. These gifts come from discriminating givers. They were made after the Institute was put to the acid test of investigation by experts in philanthropy.

When the Institute is in need, the merchant seamen who come to the port of New York are in need. Their lives have become inseparable.

Ward also made a significant contribution to the Seaman's Church through the final distribution of his will in 1960.

Tablet Erected to Commemorate the First Packard Automobile, Warren, Ohio

MODEL A
THE FIRST PACKARD

JAMES WARD PACKARD
and his brother
WILLIAM D. PACKARD
COMPLETED THEIR FIRST CAR ON THIS SITE
NOVEMBER 6, 1899

THIS TABLET PLACED FIFTY YEARS LATER BY THE PACKARD MOTOR CAR COMPANY IS A TRIBUTE TO THE INGENUITY AND PERSEVERANCE OF TWO GREAT AUTOMOTIVE PIONEERS

(This, tablet was originally placed on the wall of Packard Electric building on Dana Street. It is now housed in the National Packard Museum.)

Memorial Tablet to the Packards in Lakewood, New York

THE PACKARDS

Elizabeth Gilmer Packard
1871-1960

James Ward Packard
1863-1928

The Packards are memorialized in Lakewood for their community spirit and their generous gifts toward village improvement. They came in the late 1800's as summer visitors. After building their mansion in 1912, they became full time and enthusiastic residents.

The Village Hall, headquarters of municipal government and public safety, stands on a plat of land Mr. Packard donated to the village. He also provided partial funding for the building construction, and at its dedication in 1915 presented a Model T. chemical fire truck to the fire company. It was the company's first motorized vehicle and remains a proud artifact of its history.

The purchase of a set of carillon bells, a distinctive feature of the Lakewood Methodist Church, was made possible by a Packard gift.

Across Summit Street from the former Lakewood School, sports teams play on a field donated from Packard real estate holdings. It was dedicated as Packard Field on September 1940.

After Mr. Packard's death in 1928, Mrs. Packard remained involved in civic affairs. She served two terms on the Lakewood School Board. At the same time she created and funded scholarships for high school students, and privately supported needly individuals who wanted to further their education. Shortly before her death in 1960 Mrs. Packard made a monetary gift to the Southwestern Central School Board toward the creation of a new athletic field on that school's property.

This prominent couple, recognized for their generosity, were also regarded as good friends and neighbors. The village young people who came to know Mrs. Packard personally have especially fond memories of her cheerful personality and warm hospitality. The presence of the Packards in Lakewood has become legend.

THIS STONE MARKER IS LOCATED ON FORMER PACKARD PROPERTY,
ALONG OWANA WAY JUST SOUTH OF THE VILLAGE HALL.

Magazine Advertisement Published by the Packard Motor Car Company

This advertisement by the company was printed in various national magazines between October and December, 1928.

Appendix A
A Record of Births & Weddings

Name-Relationship	***Date Born***	***Where Born***	***Date Married***	***Who Married***	***Where Married***	***Children***
Warren Packard- Family Patriarch	*06/01/1828*	*Austintown, Ohio*	*09/21/1852*	*m1- Sylvia Camp*	*Warren, Ohio*	*-Harry -Rolla*
			11/20/1860	*m2- Mary Elizabeth Doud*	*Warren Ohio*	*-William Doud -James Ward -Alaska -Carlotta -Cornelia Olive*
William Doud Packard- Son of Warren & Mary	*11/03/1861*	*Warren, Ohio*	*06/11/1891*	*m1- Annie Storer*	*Middlesex, Connecticut*	*-Warren II*
			09/28/1906	*m2- Kathryn Bruder*	*Lakewood, New York*	*-No children*
James Ward Packard- Son of Warren & Mary	*11/05/1863*	*Warren, Ohio*	*08/31/1904*	*Elizabeth Gillmer*	*Warren, Ohio*	*-No children*
Alaska Packard- Daughter of Warren & Mary	*03/01/1868*	*Warren, Ohio*	*11/07/1893*	*m1- Ephraim Banks McCrum*	*Warren, Ohio*	*-Esther*
			07/11/1905	*m2- James B. Davidson*	*Lakewood, New York*	*-no children*
Carlotta Packard- Daughter of Warren & Mary	*04/06/1869*	*Warren, Ohio*	*Never married*			*-no children*
Cornelia Olive Packard- Daughter of Warren & Mary	*06/29/1882*	*Warren Ohio*	*06/05/1906*	*m1- Carl Foster White*	*Warren, Ohio*	*-Henry Packard*
			09/23/ 1916	*m2- Guy S. Gardner*	*Cleveland Ohio*	*-no children*
			11/23/1940	*m3- Percy W. Tinan*	*Cleveland, Ohio*	*-no children*
Warren Packard II- Son of William Doud & Annie	*10/05/1892*	*Warren, Ohio*	*08/31/1920*	*Dorothy Braden*	*Akron, Ohio*	*-Rosalie -Warren III*
Henry Packard White- Son of Carl & Olive Packard White	*04/29/1909*	*Cleveland, Ohio*	*10/20/1934*	*m1- Nancy Hutchinson Allen*	*Hamilton, Tennessee*	*-Sandra -Nancy Ann*
				m2- Frances Hershaw	*-no children*	

Appendix B
A Record of the Family's Final Resting Places

Name-Relationship	Date Died	Where Died	Cause of Death	Cemetery-City	Plot/ Grave No.
Warren Packard- Family Patriarch	07/28/1897	Warren, Ohio	Bladder Trouble	Oakwood- Warren, Ohio	O. P./ 106 & W ½ 107
Sylvia Camp- 1st Wife of Warren Packard	12/11/1856	Warren, Ohio		Oakwood- Warren, Ohio	O. P. / 106
Harry Packard- Son of Warren & Sylvia	1855	Warren, Ohio		Oakwood- Warren, Ohio	O. P. / 106
Rolla Packard- Son of Warren & Sylvia	1858	Warren, Ohio		Oakwood- Warren, Ohio	O.P. / 106
Mary Elizabeth Doud- 2nd Wife of Warren Packard	10/09/1903	Warren, Ohio	Stroke	Paltzgroff- Lordstown, Ohio	
William Doud Packard- Son of Warren & Mary	11/11/1923	Warren, Ohio	Viral Infection	Oakwood- Warren, Ohio	O. P. / E ½ 106
Annie Hadley Storer- 1st Wife of Wm. D. Packard	11/28/1895	Warren, Ohio	Appendicitis Complications	Oakwood- Warren, Ohio	O. P. / 106
Warren Packard II- Son of Wm. D. & Annie	08/26/1929	Detroit, Michigan	Airplane Accident	Oakwood- Warren, Ohio	O.P. / 106
Kathryn Bruder- 2nd Wife of Wm. D. Packard	02/10/1940	Warren, Ohio	Cerebral Hemorrhage	Oakwood- Warren, Ohio	O.P. / E ½ 106
James Ward Packard- Son of Warren & Mary	03/20/1928	Cleveland, Ohio	Abdominal Cancer	Oakwood- Warren, Ohio	Section 2/ Lot 119
Elizabeth Gillmer- Wife of James Ward Packard	01/19/1960	Lakewood, New York	Cerebral Hemorrhage	Oakwood- Warren, Ohio	Section 2/ Lot 119
Alaska Packard- Daughter of Warren & Mary	07/16/1934	Alexandria, Virginia	Surgery Complications	Paltzgroff- Lordstown, Ohio	
Ephraim Banks McCrum- 1st Husband of Alaska Packard	08/17/1908	Youngstown, Ohio	Tuberculosis	Oak Hill- Youngstown, Ohio	Row 40/ No. 26
Esther McCrum- Daughter of Alaska & Banks	04/20/1902	Columbus, Ohio	Pneumonia	Paltzgraff- Lordstown, Ohio	
James B. Davidson- 2nd Husband of Alaska Packard	05/03/1929	Alexandria, Virginia	Complications	Oakwood- Warren, Ohio	O. P. / 483
Carlotta Packard- Daughter of Warren & Mary	12/03/1940	New York, New York	Carditis	Oakwood- Warren, Ohio	O. P. / 106

Name-Relationship	Date Died	Where Died	Cause of Death	Cemetery-City	Plot/ Grave No.
Cornelia Olive Packard- Daughter of Warron & Mary	*03/09/1966*	*Cleveland, Ohio*	*Home Fire Accident*	*Lake View- Cleveland, Ohio*	*Sec. 6/ Lot. 19-B*
Carl F. White- 1st Husband of Olive Packard	*04/27/1915*	*Cleveland, Ohio*	*Pneumonia*	*Lake View- Cleveland, Ohio*	*Sec. 6/ Lot 19-B*
Henry Packard White- Son of Olive & Carl	*06/06/1974*	*Bel Air, Maryland*	*Stroke*	*Lake View- Cleveland, Ohio*	*Sec. 6/ Lot 19-B*
Guy S. Gardner 2nd Husband of Olive Packard	*03/22/1939*	*Sarasota, Florida*	*Coronary Thrombosis*	*Woodlawn- Cleveland, Ohio*	
Percy W. Tinan 3rd Husband of Olive Packard	*1953*	*Pinellas, Florida*		*Evergreen- Painesville, Ohio*	*Sec. 5A/ Row 13/#4*

NOTE: Rosalie Digby-Seymour and Warren Packard III (4th Generation), children of Warren Packard II, are also buried in the Packard family plot, Oakwood Cemetery, Warren, Ohio

Appendix C
A Record of Patents Granted to William Doud & James Ward Packard

A.-Non-Automotive Patents

Patent Number	Date Issued	Inventor	Title
383484	29/05/88	JWP	MANUFACTURE OF FILAMENTS FOR ELECTRIC LAMPS
385001	26/06/88	JWP	RHEOSTAT
390310	02/10/88	JWP	ELECTRICAL TESTING APPARATUS
391815	30/10/88	JWP	MANUFACTURE OF FILAMENTS FOR ELECTRIC LAMPS
391816	30/10/88	JWP	FLASHING APPARATUS FOR CARBON ELEMENTS
392686	13/11/88	JWP	APPARATUS FOR EXCHANGING AIR
396951	29/01/89	JWP	REVOLVING PHOTO-METER STAND
396952	29/01/89	JWP	MILLING MACHINE
401580	16/04/89	JWP	EXHAUSTING ELECTRIC LAMP BULBS
401581	16/04/89	JWP	MERCURY AIR PUMP
401582	16/04/89	JWP	VALVE ACTUATING APPARATUS
406110	02/07/89	JWP	VACUUM PUMP
417787	24/12/89	JWP	INCANDESCENT LAMP SOCKET
417788	24/12/89	JWP	INCANDESCENT LAMP SOCKET
417789	24/12/89	JWP	INCANDESCENT ELECTRIC LAMP
426055	22/04/90	JWP	INCANDESCENT ELECTRIC LAMP
426417	22/04/90	JWP	PUMP OPERATING APPARATUS
450152	14/04/91	JWP & HERROLD	VALVE FOR AIR PUMPS
496791	02/05/93	WDP	ARMATURE ATTACHMENT
511157	19/12/93	WDP	HAND REGULATOR FOR ELECTRIC MOTORS
527070	09/10/94	JWP	ELECTRICAL CONVERTER
527071	09/10/94	JWP	ELECTRICAL FUSE BOX
590852	28/09/97	JWP & WDP	ELECTRICAL TRANSFORMER
613594	01/11/98	WDP	ELECTRIC FUSE-WIRE HOLDER
628957	18/07/99	JWP	ELECTRIC TRANSFORMER
639276	19/12/99	JWP	ELECTRIC TRANSFORMER
640314	02/01/00	JWP & HWWISWELL	ELECTRIC TRANSFORMER
644330	27/02/00	JWP	ELEC. MEASURING INSTRUMENT
748781	05/01/04	WDP	ACETYLENE GAS GENERATOR
789285	09/05/05	WDP	ELECTRICAL CUT-OUT
801260	10/10/05	WDP	BASE-CUP FOR INCANDESCENT LAMP

(Patents prior to 1890 were generally assigned to Sawyer-Man, Thomson-Houston, or Westinghouse.)

B-Automotive Patents

Patent Number	Date Issued	Inventor	Title
667792	12/02/01	JWP	SPARK ADVANCE & CONTROL
667909	12/02/01	JWP & WA HATCHER	MOTOR VEHICLE FRAME
667910	12/02/01	JWP & WA HATCHER	MIXER & VAPORIZER FOR EXPLOSIVE ENGINES
694184	02/25/02	JWP & HATCHER	BRAKE WHEEL STRUCTURE
700768	27/05/02	JWP & WA HATCHER	MOTOR OILER
712583	04/11/02	JWP & WA HATCHER	CONTROLLING MECHANISM FOR MOTOR VEHICLES
712928	04/11/02	JWP & WA HATCHER	SELECTIVE TRANSMISSION & CONTROL
721912	03/03/03	JWP & WA HATCHER	RUNNING GEAR FOR MOTOR VEHICLES
722431	10/03/03	JWP	HYDROCARBON MOTOR
741365	31/10/03	JWP	SPARK IGNITER & CONTROL
749744	19/01/04	JWP & WA HATCHER	MOTOR VEHICLE
752582	16/02/04	JWP & WA HATCHER	BRAKING MECHANISM FOR MOTOR VEHICLES
769321	06/09/04	JWP	CLUTCH
773097	25/10/04	JWP & WA HATCHER	CONTROLLING MECHANISM FOR MOTOR VEHICLES
775932	29/11/04	JWP	SPARKING IGNITER DEVICE FOR HYDROCARBON ENGINES
780221	17/01/05	JWP	ELECTRIC IGNITER
787212	11/04/05	JWP	SPARKING IGNITING DEVICE FOR HYDROCARBON ENGINES
804971	21/11/05	JWP & WA	LEVER MECHANISM FOR MOTOR VEHICLES
806830	12/12/05	JWP	MIXER & VAPORIZER FOR HYDROCARBON ENGINES
830099	04/11/06	JWP	HYDROCARBON ENGINE FOR MOTOR VEHICLES
887013	05/05/08	JWP & WA	HYDROCARBON ENGINE
1022751	09/04/12	JWP	MOTOR CONTROLLING MECHANISM FOR MOTOR VEHICLES
1034728	06/08/12	JWP	WATER COOLING SYSTEM FOR HYDROCARBON ENGINES
1050288	14/01/13	JWP	VALVE OPERATING MECHANISM FOR MOTOR VEHICLES

Appendix D
A Partial Record of Packard Automobiles Owned by the Packard Family

William Doud Packard
-1900 Model A, No. A-21 (2nd Packard Built)
-1908 Model "30" Touring Car-Vehicle No. 5950
-1909 Model "18" Touring Car-Vehicle No. 9587
-1910 Model "30" Runabout-Vehicle No. 13010
-1914 Model "3-38" Phaeton-Vehicle No. 50373
-1917 Model "3-25" or "3-35" Twin Six Brougham-Motor No. 148616

James Ward Packard
-1900 Model B, No. B-29 (Supposedly Ward's personal car)
-1901 Model E, No. E-71 (Specially built for Ward)
-1913 Model "2-48" Runabout-Vehicle No. 35365
-1914 Model "2-38" Touring Car-Vehicle No. 54006
-1924 Model "226" Coupe
-1925 Model "333" Sedan-Limousine
-1925 Model "326" Coupe
-1925 Model "236" Runabout
-1926 Model "243" Club Sedan-Vehicle No. 217199
-1926 Model "433" Chassis (for mounting Phillips Custom Body)-Vehicle No. 99008

Elizabeth (Gillmer) Packard-After 1928 Death of Husband, James Ward
-1934 Model "1101" 5-Passenger Coupe-Vehicle No. 717-86
-1938 Model "1608" Touring Limousine-Vehicle No. 1135-2137
-1941 Model "1908" Touring Limousine (LeBaron)-Vehicle No. 1420-2042
-1956 Model "5682" Patrician Sedan-Vehicle No. 5682-1541

Warren Packard II
-1909 Model "18" Roadster-Vehicle No. 9673
-1929 Monobloc Twelve Experimental Car-used by Warren II for a period of time during 1929

Index